SHE CAN'T STOP
MILEY
CYRUS
THE BIOGRAPHY

SHE CAN'T STOP
MILEY
CYRUS

THE BIOGRAPHY

SARAH OLIVER

JOHN BLAKE

Published by John Blake Publishing Ltd,
3 Bramber Court, 2 Bramber Road,
London W14 9PB, England

www.johnblakepublishing.co.uk

www.facebook.com/Johnblakepub 🖪
twitter.com/johnblakepub 🖪

This edition published in 2014

ISBN: 978 1 78219 992 2

British Library Cataloguing-in-Publication Data:

A catalogue record for this book is available from the British Library.

Design by www.envydesign.co.uk

Printed and bound in Great Britain by CPI Group (UK) Ltd

1 3 5 7 9 10 8 6 4 2

Papers used by John Blake Publishing are natural, recyclable products made
from wood grown in sustainable forests. The manufacturing processes
conform to the environmental regulations of the country of origin.

Every attempt has been made to contact the relevant copyright-holders,
but some were unobtainable. We would be grateful if the appropriate
people could contact us.

CONTENTS

CHAPTER ONE

1992: A STAR IS BORN

On 23 November 1992 Tish Finley gave birth to a little girl. She was overjoyed that the baby had arrived safely as she was quite a few weeks early. Her partner, Billy Ray Cyrus, the baby's dad, wasn't by her side because he was a famous country singer and was away touring the USA and Europe. His number-one single 'Achy Breaky Heart' had been released just a few months earlier. It had topped the charts in America, Canada and Australia, earning Billy Ray worldwide fame. He had planned some time off around Tish's due date in December but because of complications the doctors had had to bring the birth forward.

Billy Ray found out by fax that Tish had given birth and rushed as fast as he could to the hospital. Both Tish and the baby needed extra care from the hospital's medical team and they had to wait eight days before they could go home.

They chose to give the baby the name Destiny Hope because they felt she was destined for great things. She was a little sister for Brandi and Trace, who were Tish's children from a previous relationship. Billy Ray explained on *Piers Morgan Tonight*, 'You know, [Miley's] name was originally Destiny Hope. I had given her the name before she was born because I had a vision. I felt it was her destiny to bring hope to the world.

'When I see her selling out arenas around the world or on her TV show, making people laugh, bringing families into the living room together, we always, you know, try to put positive messages in each episode if we could. And you know, I do think that she – this is her purpose – her path.'

Miley was born into a complicated mess. Billy Ray had met Tish while he was still married to his wife Cindy, although they had an amicable divorce soon afterwards. Billy Ray and Tish met in July 1991 and started out as friends. Brandi was only four and Trace was just two at the time. As their relationship developed they fell deeply in love and were so happy when Tish fell pregnant.

However, just a few months before Billy Ray met Tish he had had a brief relationship with a Kristen Luckey, a waitress he'd met at one of his gigs, and in April 1993 she gave birth to a bouncing baby boy. She named him Christopher Cody. The fact that both Tish and Kristen had been pregnant at the same time had the potential to cause great harm to Billy Ray's singing career so it was kept hush-hush for as long as possible.

Billy Ray and Tish got married on 28 December 1993, when Miley was one and Tish was pregnant with their son Braison. Billy Ray wanted to commit completely to Tish and knew that marriage was something she really wanted.

Billy Ray didn't talk about his secret son in interviews but the week after Miley turned two he was on a Tennessee show called *Music City Tonight*. One of the show's hosts knew that Billy Ray had got Tish and the other woman pregnant at the same time so asked him about it. He didn't know what to say but then Miley toddled onto the set pushing a pram and saved the day. All the focus centred on her and Billy Ray could rest easy.

Destiny was a very happy baby and was always smiling and cooing. Because of this Billy Rae and Tish decided to give her the nickname 'Smiley' and they soon discovered they were calling her Smiley more than Destiny. Shortly before she started at school they decided that they couldn't call her Smiley anymore because other children in her class might tease her for it so they shortened it to Miley. From that day onwards Destiny/Smiley has been known as Miley. She made it legally her name in January 2008 when she was fifteen, choosing to add the middle name 'Ray' in memory of her granddad.

DID YOU KNOW?
The only person who still calls Miley by her birth name is her grandma.

Miley was so excited when Braison was born on 9 May 1994. Now she had a little brother to play with. The Cyrus family was completed six years later when Tish gave birth to another little girl on 8 January 2000. They named her Noah.

The Cyrus children are all very close, thanks in part to growing up on an isolated Tennessee farm. They couldn't nip to their friends' houses to play so instead had to play with each other, playing games and making dens. They also played with their pets and animals on the farm, as Miley explained to Office Max during a Q&A session with fans in December 2007: 'I have lots of horses, kitty cats, dogs, chickens and fish. My dogs are on tour with me. We love animals. My dad had a pet squirrel for a while that kept coming around. He loves animals, too [laughs]. He makes eggs and bacon every morning for my dogs.'

Whenever Billy Ray came home from touring and gigging he made sure to make a big fuss of Miley and her siblings and, in many ways, he was more of a friend to them than a father. He wasn't very strict and never smacked his children. Miley knew that her dad was different to her friends' fathers but as a young child she couldn't understand what being famous meant. When she was less than a year old, she would toddle onto the stage while he was performing and wave at the thousands of people in the audience. As soon as she was talking she began to sing along with Billy Ray. He was very proud of her and, when she was six, he let her be in his music videos; something that Miley really enjoyed.

DID YOU KNOW?

Now and again, when little Miley was on stage with her dad, she would search through the bras and pants thrown on stage for him and find the biggest pair. She would then tell him she'd found his biggest fan!

Miley went to Heritage Elementary School in Spring Hill, Tennessee, which is where she began to develop her own performing skills. She enjoyed being in school productions, even though she wasn't given the lead roles, and in the school holidays she went to an acting camp. She also followed in the footsteps of her mum in joining a competitive cheerleading squad. The older girls in the Premier Tennessee Allstars squad looked out for her and they had great fun travelling all around America for different competitions. She is still friends with some of her teammates today.

Miley revealed to *TeenMag* in 2009, 'When we would go on trips with my cheerleading team, we would always sing and do karaoke. So I've always been performing.'

She confided in a separate interview with journalist David Hiltbrand, 'The training is pretty harsh but it's so worth it once you're on stage and getting trophies.'

At school Miley enjoyed learning different languages but she hated Maths class.

DID YOU KNOW?

Miley wasn't all sweet and innocent; she was kicked out of one private evangelical school for being rebellious. She had explained what French kissing was to the other girls and had stolen her teacher's mobility scooter. This was kept a secret from the press for a long time and Miley only admitted to it when she was twenty.

By the time she was eight years old Miley had decided that she wanted to be a professional actress when she grew up. Her dad remembers the exact moment she decided, explaining to the *San Francisco Chronicle*, 'We saw the play *Mamma Mia!*, and halfway through it Miley nudged me and said, "This is what I want to do. I want to be a great actress."'

Her family encouraged her to pursue her acting ambitions because they knew it was what she wanted but Billy Ray would have been happy if she'd just been a normal student instead. She ended up having to leave cheerleading behind her when she started auditioning. Miley admitted in an interview with BMI.com in December 2007 that she used to put on her own shows for her family, saying, 'When I was little, I would stand up on couches and say, "Watch me." We had these showers that are completely glass, and I would lock people in them and make them stay in there and watch me perform. I'd make them watch.'

Miley has many fond memories of growing up on the farm but in school things were difficult for her and she has fewer happy memories. Other children were jealous of her because she had a famous father and had money so they enjoyed teasing Miley and making her unhappy. She had to deal with lots of bullies and would often burst into tears because of the cruel things they said to her. It must have been so hard for Miley to cope as even her so-called friends would turn on her and enjoy making her life a misery. One day the bullies thought it would be fun to lock her in the bathroom – they really were horrible girls – but Miley was so scared she didn't dare tell an adult. Things only improved when her dad overheard her talking about what the bullies had done to her on the phone and decided to go and speak to the school principal.

When the school investigated what had been going on they discovered that Miley had been putting up with abuse for a long time and it was suggested that it might be a good idea to involve the police but Miley didn't want to do that – she just wanted to leave the school and forget about the bullies and their taunts. From then on she was home schooled, which was so much better for her. She talked about the girls who bullied her in an interview on *The View* talk show, saying, 'They were the bigger girls. They were like, "We'll keep you safe if you're not friends with Miley," [to the other girls in Miley's class]. I remember this one day: it was lunch time and we had assigned seats because things were getting that out of control that people weren't even allowed to sit near each other and there was assigned-seat day, but wherever you sat, that was where you were for the rest of the year... and no one sat by me, so for the rest of the year I sat alone every day. That's the scariest part, just being alone.'

In a separate interview with chat-show host and model Tyra Banks, Miley explained how the bullies knocked her confidence. She revealed,

I remember when I was in school, they had this picture of me that was seriously the worst picture of me you've ever seen. I was always really little and I remember going to the gym one day and we all had to get weighed, which first of all I just don't like that anyway because I don't think you should have to get weighed in front of your peers, and it just makes girls uncomfortable. And I was always smaller than everyone else and I remember them being like, 'Ah, she's so small.' I think that's when it was really like 'We can get her' type thing. And there was this picture of me where I was just so little. I was standing next to them and you could really see the contrast. They had it on their binder every day and they were, like, showing me the picture of us standing beside each other, trying to scare me, and when you really look at it, it's scary. Scary thoughts.

DID YOU KNOW?

When she was in *Hannah Montana*, Miley had a tutor and in the breaks in between shooting each season she went to a special school called Options For Youth. The students there either had a one-to-one tutor or were in a small group and shared a tutor.

Miley still receives abuse today from bloggers who enjoy saying nasty things about the way she looks. She tends not to read what they write but sometimes offending articles do catch her eye. After some bloggers wrote that she had 'jiggling thighs' she decided to hit back in a series of tweets. Miley wrote,

Talk all you want. I have my flaws. I'm a normal girl, there's things about my body I would change but stop with calling me f*t in post. I don't even like the word. Those remarks that you hateful people use are fighting words. The ones that scar people and cause them to do damage to themselves or others.

People that are so okay with being so hateful disgust me and need to spend less time on a gossip website and more time a. reading your Bible, b. reading stories/articles about what happens when cyber abuse and name calling happens. Kids hurt themselves. This is not something to be taken lightly. I know these 'message boards' are 'no big deal' to YOU but it is to the victim. This has got to stop!!!

Oh and P.S. if your thighs don't jiggle go see a doctor. Thanks.

Miley ended her final tweet with a link to a cyber-bullying website so that anyone receiving online abuse could get help and advice.

DID YOU KNOW?

Miley's godmother might be Dolly Parton but the first CD she ever bought was Britney Spears' 'Hit Me Baby One More Time'. She had no idea back then that she would end up recording a track with Britney in 2013.

DID YOU KNOW?

Miley was born left-handed like her dad, but when she was a child, Billy Ray taught her how to write with her right hand instead. She explained why during a Moviefone interview: 'My dad was like, "You shouldn't be left-handed... you'll have to learn the world backwards so you need to learn to write with your right hand," and so I started to be right-handed.'

Miley first learnt to play the guitar left-handed and then she decided to learn it right-handed, so now she can do both.

CHAPTER TWO

'DADDY, I WANT TO BE AN ACTRESS!'

Miley didn't spend all of her childhood on the farm in Tennessee as life changed for the Cyrus family in the early 2000s when Billy Ray's popularity waned. His music career stalled so he decided to listen to some advice that his dad had given him a few years before. Billy Ray explained to the *San Francisco Chronicle*, 'He said, "Son, I think you have all your eggs in one basket with this music. I think you should branch out into one of those Kenny Rogers or Dolly Parton careers." The next week, while I was touring in Los Angeles, I read in a newspaper about a casting call for David Lynch's *Mulholland Drive*. My agent helped get me an audition, and lo and behold, they hired me.'

Shortly after finishing *Mulholland Drive* Billy Ray got the lead part in the sitcom *Doc*, which was filmed in Toronto, Canada. Miley must have been thrilled because she got to see what it was like to be an actor and it meant that she could move far away from the bullies.

Miley was determined to be an actress but her first audition happened quite by accident. She had decided to go to see some friends audition for a TV advert for Banquet Foods so that she would have some idea of what to expect when she went to an audition of her own. But instead of observing her friends, she ended up auditioning herself. Her friends were too young for the part but their mum suggested that Miley take the opportunity and she performed wonderfully. The people casting the advert were so impressed with Miley that they offered her the part. If you want to see the advert, just go to YouTube and search for Miley Cyrus Banquet Foods advert.

Miley's first proper acting job came in 2001 while she was living in Toronto with her family. She loved spending time on the set of *Doc* with her dad and would chat with the cast and crew while she was there. Each week she would always ask her dad if he had got his new script and ask if she had been given a part. One day her wish to be in *Doc* came true when she was asked whether she would like to appear in an episode. She jumped at the chance and put everything she had into playing a character called Kiley, who had just moved with her dad into the same apartment block as Doc (played by Billy Ray). Miley got such a buzz from being in front of the camera that it made her want to be an actress even more.

Miley might have had raw ability but, if she wanted to succeed, she knew she had to take as many acting classes as possible so that she could become even better and make herself stand out in auditions. She knew that she would be competing with girls who had been acting for years but she was more than up for the challenge. When her Toronto friends were building snowmen or sledging, she just wanted to be in a theatre practising every minute she could. She wanted to get a role because of her acting skills, not because she was Billy Ray's daughter.

When she was growing up, Miley really fancied the country singer George Strait, who used to wear a huge cowboy hat all the time. His nickname was the 'King of Country' and her grandma had a huge crush on him too. He is 40 years older than Miley but that didn't matter to her when she was singing along to his songs in the car on the way to the *Doc* set. She would have loved to marry him!

Her other childhood crush was the group Hanson. She went to see them perform live with her big sister Brandi and they waited outside their tour bus just to try to catch a glimpse of them. Lots of girls in Miley's school fancied Isaac, Taylor and Zac so she wasn't alone. The boys might have been older than her but only by ten or so years.

One of her first love interests was a boy called Tyler Posey. She met him on the set of *Doc* and gave him his first kiss. Tyler told *Seventeen* magazine, 'We dated for two years and broke up when we were eleven. I saw her three years later on TV, and freaked out! We're still friends.'

DID YOU KNOW?

Tyler is best known for playing Scott McCall in the MTV show *Teen Wolf* and the young son of Jennifer Lopez's character Marisa in the blockbuster *Maid in Manhattan*.

In 2003, when Miley was eleven, she was cast in the Tim Burton movie *Big Fish*. It was a huge deal as it was a Hollywood blockbuster that would be shown all around the world. There were so many famous actors and actresses in the movie: Ewan McGregor, Helena Bonham Carter, Danny DeVito... and it was being directed by Tim Burton, who had directed *Planet of the Apes* and *Batman Returns*. Miley was playing the part of an eight-year-old girl called Ruthie. She only had to say, 'Edward, don't,' to a boy as he made his way to the witch's house but it was still a talking role so was better than being an extra.

The movie was filmed 800 miles away from Toronto in Montgomery and Wetumpka, Alabama, so Miley had to travel a long way to film her scene. Her first taste of being a film star wasn't at all glamorous; her scene was set in a swamp at night so there were loads of creepy crawlies and it was very cold. Despite this, she loved the experience of being in a film and having that under her belt surely boosted her chances at future auditions.

As well as filming *Big Fish* in 2003 Miley auditioned for a brand-new Disney TV show, which was to be called *Hannah Montana*. The audition process was complicated and for a long time Miley didn't know if she would be chosen to play the lead role of a schoolgirl who has a double life as a worldwide recording artist. She revealed to the *Daily Mail*, 'When I originally auditioned for the show I was eleven and I didn't get the role till I was thirteen, so it was two years of waiting and wondering if it was ever going to happen for me. It was heartbreaking, thinking I wasn't going to get it and my father kept saying, "You know, Miley, you've got all the time in the world – take your time and just be a kid," but this was all I ever wanted to do. I wanted to live my dream and I'm just glad everything's finally worked out.'

When Miley had first auditioned for *Hannah Montana*, she tried out for the part of Lilly Truscott but deep down she knew she wanted to play Chloe Stewart. Later, when she got the part, they changed the character's name to Miley Stewart to make it less confusing – otherwise Miley would have been acting as Chloe, who is also Hannah!

The first step in the audition process involved Miley's agent sending Disney a tape of Miley reading Lilly's lines. They were so impressed that they asked for another tape, this time of Miley reading Chloe Stewart's lines. Miley explained to Zap2it, 'I did taping. I did two tapes, four tapes. I started out as Lilly and they wanted me to audition for Hannah Montana and that sounded very positive. They said, "You are too small, too young. Bye-bye." Well, that's rude. So I made another tape. Dang it! They are going to watch my tape and like it!'

One day, out of the blue, when Miley had almost given up hope, she got a call from the people casting *Hannah Montana*, asking her to fly out for a face-to-face audition in Los Angeles. Her dream of playing Chloe wasn't over!

Miley knew that she had to put everything into the audition. She knew that Disney had thought that she might be too young to play Chloe so she decided to wear make-up and her mum's high heels to make herself look older. When she arrived at the audition, she saw that there were lots of other girls she would have to beat to get the part. 'The audition process for anything is so scary. You walk into a room with sixty girls. In my case, I have to say, if I was them I don't know why they chose me. You can see their head shots and just know they know a lot more than you do. They don't like you – that is the scariest part!' she explained to Zap2it.

Miley's audition went really well but it wasn't until two weeks later that she found out she'd got down to the final thirty girls. After impressing again she was told she was down to the final three. Her last audition was so tough because the other two girls were super-talented. Miley must have been so happy when she was told she was the girl they wanted to play Chloe. She'd had such a long time to wait: she was eleven when she had her first audition and she filmed her first episode of *Hannah Montana* when she was thirteen!

The show's creators had, in fact, been blown away in the audition room but it had taken a while for them to come to the decision to hire Miley because she was so young and inexperienced. The other two girls in the final three had much more experience. One of the girls was sixteen, so three full years older than Miley, and the other one was Taylor Momsen, who'd been in the movie *Spy Kids 2*. When they were weighing up which girl would be best for the job, they realised that Miley's dad was Billy Ray Cyrus. Before she got down to the final three no one from Disney knew who her dad was because Billy Ray believed it important that Miley should get the job because of her own talents, not because she was his daughter.

The creators realised that Miley might have star quality in her genes. They took a chance on her because they wanted to see the magic they'd seen in the audition rooms on TV. They also managed to convince Disney bosses that she was the perfect choice. Miley told Jonathan Ross on his talk show, 'Five minutes before my audition, I spilt Dr Pepper on me and a bird pooped on my head, and apparently that's good luck because I got the part.'

When Billy Ray knew that things were going to change because Miley was to play Hannah Montana, he wrote a song about how he was feeling. Called 'Ready Set Don't Go', it was about the moment when a father knows he's got to let his daughter go. In the song, Billy Ray talks about Miley having ambitions bigger than her town and how she's waiting for his blessing before she can go. It explains how he uses a smile to cover his broken heart and that he's got to let her spread her wings. It's a powerful song, full of raw emotion.

DID YOU KNOW?

If you want to see Miley's auditions for yourself, you should check them out on YouTube. Just search for 'Miley Cyrus Hannah Montana audition'. You can see Miley's first audition and later ones with her acting and singing alongside her dad. They're great to watch and show why she was picked.

The man behind *Hannah Montana* was Gary Marsh, Disney Channel's President of Entertainment. He decided a show like *Hannah Montana* had to be made because Disney was making normal kids into huge acting stars and then once they left, they were becoming huge recording artists. People like Britney Spears, Justin Timberlake and Christina Aguilera all started out on Disney shows. Gary told *Variety*, 'We drove these kids into giant success stories... but we thought, "Shouldn't we be growing this internally?" We were making celebrities out of other people's rock stars.'

Gary was very involved in the process to find the right girl to play Hannah Montana and he knew Miley desperately wanted to play her after her first audition. He also got his wish of 'growing someone internally': Miley became the first artist to have television, film, consumer products and music deals with Disney.

He explained to *Knight Ridder Newspapers* what made her stand out: 'We got a call from an agent [who said], "Miley will fly herself out to audition again." Let me tell you, we've done a lot of auditions over the years, and no one has ever made that offer before. I said, "We have to see this girl again."'

Once Miley got the part of Hannah Montana, Billy Ray decided that he wanted to try out for the part of Robbie Stewart, Miley's dad in the show. He didn't know if he was good enough but he wanted to give it a try. It was the first time he'd considered acting again since his show *Doc* but he knew acting alongside Miley would be amazing.

Billy Ray explains, 'When I left *Doc*, I said I will never do another TV series. I really missed making music and being with my fans... Then this opportunity came up – such a great script, the opportunity to be in business with such a great company as Disney, and then, the icing on the cake, to get to work and experience this with my daughter.'

Billy Ray approached Steve Peterman and the rest of the *Hannah Montana* creators and asked for an audition. At first they weren't sure because they wanted an experienced comedy actor to play Robbie. They knew that Billy Ray hadn't done that much acting before but they decided it wouldn't do any harm if they gave him an audition because, after all, he was Miley's dad. They weren't expecting anything great but when they compared his audition with the other two dads who had been shortlisted for the part, there was one clear winner – Billy Ray. They liked the way he and Miley joked around and interacted with each other, and the fact that he could play the guitar and sing was a huge bonus.

Miley was so happy when she was told that Billy Ray would be playing her dad in *Hannah Montana* because it meant that they would be spending a lot of time together. If he hadn't got the part, he might have had to live separately from the rest of the family. Having Billy Ray work with her every day would make her feel loved and protected and she could ask him for advice whenever she needed it.

CHAPTER THREE

JUST CALL
ME HANNAH

The whole Cyrus family needed to uproot to Los Angeles ASAP so Tish picked their first Los Angeles home off the Internet and bought it without even viewing it in person. She just liked the photos on the website and knew it would be a nice place to live. There wasn't the time to spend looking at various properties; she just needed somewhere they could move straight into.

Once Miley had signed her contract she had to start developing her two characters and master learning lots of lines in a limited amount of time. In each episode she had so many lines that it was really important that she knew the scripts inside out. She explained what it was like playing a character leading a double life to TV critic David Kronke:

As an actor, it's really fun, because you get to experience different things from different perspectives. As a person, it's a little harder. It's double the work – not only for me, but for the wardrobe people, the hair and make-up people and everyone else. It's hard but really fun to be the character.

The cool part is I've gotten to add my own take to it. I relate to both of them so easily. I take the script in, but it's important to be myself. I didn't want to make a big fake persona, because the script calls for a real girl. So my being from Tennessee with no experience worked to my advantage – they got the normal, average girl and turned me into a pop star.

DID YOU KNOW?

Originally the show wasn't going to be called *Hannah Montana*. The writing team came up with a whole host of other names for Miley's rock-star alter ego, including Anna Cabana, Samantha York and Alexis Texas. Those names seem weird now as no one can imagine any name other than Hannah Montana as the lead character and show title.

Before *Hannah Montana* aired for the first time Miley had to perform on stage in front of 700 kids so that it could be filmed for the show. Her first concert was one of the most nerve-wracking things she has ever done. No one in the audience had any idea who Miley was – they were just encouraged to go to the free concert and get the chance to appear on TV.

Miley was given just four days to prepare six songs with a singing coach and a choreographer. She couldn't back out and she couldn't have her dad on stage with her; she just had to go out on her own and do her best. She was expecting nothing from the audience except silence – but she was in for a big shock. They loved her! They chanted 'Hannah, Hannah!' and screamed and cheered for her. It was the same kind of reaction Britney Spears or Beyoncé would get. From that moment on Miley was a star and Disney bosses knew that they had struck gold.

When the *Hannah Montana* pilot aired a few months later, it was a huge hit. It premiered on 24 March 2006 to the largest audience ever recorded for a Disney Channel show – 5.4 million!

DID YOU KNOW?

Miley likes watching old episodes and remembering what it was like when she was starting out. The show's writers used some of Miley's real-life experiences when writing the scripts so watching these episodes brings back even more memories of growing up in the Cyrus family.

Working with her dad wasn't all plain sailing for Miley. Sometimes he really embarrassed her, as she explained to journalist Maya Motavalli: 'When we're doing photo shoots or something, he'll just yell out things I wouldn't want anyone to know, just random stuff. "Remember that time when you were a kid?", that kind of stuff. But it's funny. It breaks the ice. It makes everyone smile. If it takes embarrassing me to make everyone happy, I'll take it.'

When Billy Ray was asked by the *San Francisco Chronicle* about the pros and cons of working so closely with Miley, he said, 'It's give and take all the way. It's a fine line, and sometimes it feels like I'm walking it suspended between two of the tallest buildings in New York City. I take one step at a time. Trust me: whether it's work or personal, sometimes things just get off balance. If I step in the wrong direction, I just try and step back. The most important law is to stay Miley's best friend. We came into this thing as best friends. The most important thing is to keep it that way.'

DID YOU KNOW?

When Miley first started acting, she tried to lose her accent because there weren't many parts that required girls to have southern accents. When cast as Hannah, she went with her new-and-improved accent but Disney didn't like it. They wanted the real Miley and her Tennessee accent. Miley quickly went back to using her real accent and that is the voice she uses in her TV shows and movies.

When she was growing up, Jesus was the number-one man in Miley's life. She loved talking about her faith and wanted to inspire her fans to pick up a Bible and get to know him.

She might not have been a preacher like her great-grandfather Eldon Cyrus but she wanted to be a light in the darkness. Her dad is a strong Christian too and echoed Miley's beliefs when he told *Today's Christian* magazine, 'I am at peace with my life – past, present and future. I know all things that are good come from Almighty God above. I count my blessings every single day. Every day I pray God will show me the doors He wants me to walk through, the people He wants me to talk to, the songs He wants me to sing. I want to be the light He wants me to be in this world.'

Miley echoed his thoughts when she spoke to *FOX News* in March 2008: 'I think it's my faith that keeps me grounded, especially because I'm a Christ follower, for sure. Live like Christ and he'll live in you and that's what I want to do.'

Miley and her family went to church every Sunday and then just spent the rest of the day chilling out together because there was no *Hannah Montana* filming on Sundays. But Miley knew that being a Christian is more than just going church on a Sunday: she tried to pray and read her Bible every day. At first she and her family just went to church because they liked it; they didn't have a relationship with Jesus. This changed when they joined The People's Church in Franklin. Suddenly, things slotted into place and they started to put God first in their lives.

DID YOU KNOW?

The whole family was baptised before they left Tennessee and moved to Los Angeles.

Miley loved reading her Bible and would stay up late at night reading it sometimes. She and her family believe that the Bible is different from any other book in the world because you can read it a hundred times and you'd still learn something new each time. She explained to *TV Guide*: 'It's my "how-to" guide for life.'

Miley's Bible has helped her through some tough times. She especially liked reading the Book of Psalms, which are songs and poems of praise to God. Reading the Book of Psalms helped her cope with being bullied, deal with her heart condition tachycardia and learn that money doesn't matter, she says. She told *TV Guide*, 'I don't know what I would do without a God that blesses me with the ability to do this.'

Miley was very happy to be a virgin and vowed to remain one until her wedding day but as she grew older her feelings changed. She had worn a purity ring on her ring finger to symbolise the promise she made to herself, her family and God but she took it off once she had changed her mind.

Miley's first proper kiss was on the set of *Hannah Montana*. She was really nervous because she'd never done it before but the boy she had to kiss mistook her nerves and thought she was nervous because she might be a bad kisser. Although she never names him in interviews she says that he taught her how to kiss. After the cameras stopped rolling she said bye and ran off. It must have been weird having to share your first kiss with a room full of people.

Miley has had quite a few on-screen kisses. When filming *Hannah Montana* she never got to pick who she was going to kiss, she was just told who her love interests would be. You would have thought she'd have been embarrassed kissing boys with her dad nearby but she wasn't: she saw on-screen kisses as being part of the job and not the same as kissing boys in real life.

DID YOU KNOW?

When filming *Hannah Montana* Miley's favourite foods were pizza (barbecue chicken) and the Spanish dish of eggs with fries. She loved tomato ketchup so much that she used to drink it straight from the bottle!

Playing Hannah Montana didn't just give Miley the opportunity to act, it also gave her the chance to sing. Miley released several Hannah Montana albums during her time on the show, which made her very happy to begin with. As time went by she just wanted to record her own music rather than sing songs she wasn't passionate about, though. She didn't want to be controlled and wanted to do things her own way.

Her first album was called simply *Hannah Montana* and it was released on 24 October 2006. Number 1 in the USA, number 7 in the UK and number 10 in Canada, it was filled with tracks that she sings on the show.

Track Listing:
1. The Best of Both Worlds
2. Who Said
3. Just Like You
4. Pumpin' Up the Party
5. If We Were a Movie
6. I Got Nerve
7. The Other Side of Me
8. This Is the Life
9. Pop Princess

10. She's No You
11. Find Yourself in You
12. Shining Star
13. I Learned from You
    Special Edition Bonus Track:
14. Nobody's Perfect

Miley's second album was released eight months later on 26 June 2007. *Hannah Montana 2: Meet Miley Cyrus* was number 1 in America, number 3 in Canada, number 8 in the UK and did well in other countries too. It was a double album, with the first disc being the soundtrack to the second series of *Hannah Montana* and the second disc being Miley's own music.

Track Listing:
Disc 1
1. We Got the Party
2. Nobody's Perfect
3. Make Some Noise
4. Rock Star
5. Old Blue Jeans
6. Life's What You Make It
7. One In a Million
8. Bigger Than Us
9. You and Me Together
10. True Friend
Disc 2
1. See You Again
2. East Northumberland High

3. Let's Dance
4. G.N.O (Girl's Night Out)
5. Right Here
6. As I Am
7. Start All Over
8. Clear
9. Good and Broken
10. I Miss You

Miley had always said that music was the love of her life so she was over the moon when she was told that one of the discs would be her own music. She was so proud of the ten songs she worked on for it, telling Walmart Soundcheck,

My Miley album is a little different from *Hannah Montana* because I wrote a lot of the songs on the album and I think that makes it more personal, and the title of the album is *Meet Miley Cyrus* and that's exactly what this album is. It's meeting me and introducing myself and what I've gone through more than just the *Hannah Montana* thing.

My *Meet Miley Cyrus* stuff is kind of rock'n'roll and then it's also got a little bit of a pop vibe which is kind of, it's very meeting me, meeting my style. I mean some things are more techno, and some things have lots of guitar, it's so weird like you've kind of got to listen to the music to understand. There's no way to give it a certain style.

In January 2013, when Miley was twenty, she reflected on the past and told *Cosmopolitan* what it had been like releasing her *Hannah Montana* albums. She confessed, 'Disney's always been on my back saying, "You've got to promote the TV show in two months, so make sure your record's done... and when you promote your record, can you promote the show, the movie, and the *Hannah Montana* record?" I was basically carrying two people's careers and trying to make mine the priority.'

When Miley was working on *Hannah Montana*, she was secretly dating Nick Jonas for a while but had to come clean in the end. They carried on dating for a couple of years and then they split. Poor Miley was heartbroken. They eventually put the split behind them and tried to be good friends.

They might have dated when they were only thirteen/ fourteen but Miley believes that she and Nick were both very mature because they were growing up in show business and had albums and shows to promote all the time. They both wanted to be the best performers they could and wanted their records to do really well. It was tough with them both being big stars because one day she would be in Germany, the next Nick would be somewhere else, so it was difficult for them to be in the same place at the same time and to be able to chill out together without the interruption of work commitments. Nick is Miley's first love and she says she will always love him with all of her being.

In an interview with Amanda de Cadenet on *The Conversation* Miley admitted, 'I had my biggest heartbreak when I was fourteen even though that sounds crazy, because I was fourteen, but that's what love was to me.

'I was in love with somebody. I was in love with this person that I thought was so perfect and so amazing, so when you get your heart broken that's all you see. I'm like, "The rest of my life is ruined because he doesn't love me back... He doesn't think I'm pretty, then I'm not pretty, he doesn't think I'm worth his time, I'm not worth anyone's time."'

'Going through that with your daughter is really, really hard, especially for Miley being on tour,' Tish told E! 'There were times when I was like, "Oh my gosh, I just wish we were home and she could just kind of get over this in private."'

Miley decided to be honest with her fans and let them know how she was feeling during the weeks that followed her split from Nick. She was able to show them that just because a relationship breaks down it doesn't mean that you'll never be happy again. Miley cried for a month and dyed her hair black to rebel against Nick because he liked her hair just the way it was. Now it probably seems childish to Miley but back then it allowed her to move forwards.

She revealed all about their romance to *Seventeen* magazine: 'We became boyfriend and girlfriend the day we met. He was on a quest to meet me, and he was like, "I think you're beautiful and I really like you." And I was like, "Oh my gosh, I like you so much."

'For two years he was basically my 24/7. But it was really hard to keep it from people. We were arguing a lot, and it really wasn't fun.'

During Miley's *Hannah Montana* days she was close to the other Disney kids – people like Vanessa Hudgens, Demi Lovato and Ashley Tisdale. She was also close to actresses and singers Aly and AJ Michalka. The sisters now record under their band name 78violet.

Her best friend was a girl called Vanessa, whom Miley first met when she was visiting sick children in a Los Angeles hospital. Vanessa was only nine when they met for the first time and Miley felt a connection to her straight away. She wanted to get to know Vanessa properly and invited her to visit her on the set of *Hannah Montana*. Vanessa had cystic fibrosis and was very ill. She couldn't do everything a normal nine-year-old girl could do but she still smiled. They became best friends and Vanessa helped Miley realise how precious life is and that her problems were small compared to those of people who are seriously ill. Sadly, Vanessa passed away three years after they met.

Miley was devastated when Vanessa died because she thought she would have many more years with her. She told the *Daily Mail* in an interview, 'Last year I lost one of my closest friends to cystic fibrosis. She was almost 13 and she passed away while I was on tour so I couldn't go back home when it happened. I kind of went crazy. I couldn't understand why it had happened and I was really upset.

'I was touring with the Jonas Brothers and Nick said I had to pull myself together, and he was right because I was going mad.'

After Vanessa died Miley became close to dancer Mandy Jiroux. She was five years older than Miley but it didn't affect their friendship since Miley was very mature for her age. Mandy had been one of Miley's *Hannah Montana* dancers for many years. In February 2008 they posted a funny video on their own YouTube channel after Miley got a new computer. Their first video was a big hit with Miley's fans so they decided to film more. The first four episodes of *The Miley and Mandy Show* were viewed by more than a million people (in total) in just a few weeks. To think it all started because Miley got a new computer. They thoroughly enjoyed picking the music and filming the videos in Miley's bedroom. Then Miley edited it all together into a great episode.

DID YOU KNOW?

It was through watching *The Miley and Mandy Show* that Miley's fans started to call themselves Smilers. Mandy would call Miley 'Milers' and 'Smilers' during the different episodes.

As time went on, Mandy became like a sister to Miley and they started wearing matching 'Life's Good' bracelets. Being Miley's best friend made Mandy a kind of celebrity herself because *The Miley and Mandy Show* videos on YouTube were viewed by so many people. The girls would go shopping, have a sleepover and film their show. There was a time when they were filming videos together every other day.

Miley inspired Mandy to take up singing and she joined a girl group called The Beach Girl5. They posted their last video on 6 September 2009 and Miley's fans were gutted; they had no way of keeping up-to-date with Miley and Mandy's friendship and after a while Mandy slipped off the radar. Mandy's fans didn't realise it but she was busy touring with her band around the world. Mandy revealed all in a video she posted on the Miley Mandy YouTube channel on 15 November 2013. She looked very different as her brown locks had gone and she had blonde hair. 'It's been five years since a video was uploaded to mileymandy YouTube channel... Crazy!' she said.

She revealed that for four of the years she had been in her girl group but had spent the last year dancing and choreographing for American rapper and producer Sky Blu. Mandy said that she was very proud of Miley, who was on her Bangerz Tour at the time the video was posted. Using the name MJX, Mandy had launched a solo career. Her first dance single, 'Speakers Boom', was available for download on iTunes on 10 May 2013.

For more information on Mandy and her music, visit www.mjx.fm or add her on Twitter @MandyJiroux. She is still friends with Miley but they aren't as close as they used to be, no doubt due to them both being busy touring and doing their own thing.

DID YOU KNOW?

Miley was good friends with actress and model Brenda Song for a long time when she was dating Miley's brother Trace. Taylor Swift was also a good friend of Miley's when she was starting out but they grew apart.

Miley was devastated when her email account was hacked in 2007 and her private photographs were posted online. In them, she was revealing her stomach and posing in her knickers while blowing kisses at the camera. This caused Miley a lot of heartache as she had never wanted the photos to go public and people criticised her for taking them in the first place because she was only in her early teens.

The hacker was a teenager called Josh Holly, who thought he would never be caught and was so confident that he gave anonymous interviews to websites. He told the website Threat Level that he had hacked into Miley's email account messagemebaby@gmail.com and found the photos, which had been sent to Nick Jonas when Miley was dating him.

Josh had wanted to sell the photos so had contacted the celebrity-gossip website TMZ.com, among others, but they had flatly refused because they had been gained illegally. In the end, because he couldn't make any money, he decided to publish them at digitalgangster.com for the world to see. Some celebrity websites then reposted the images for free and wrote sensationalised stories to accompany them. They had no regard for Miley's feelings at all.

Josh was thrown when he was tracked down and his apartment was raided in October 2007. He was arrested for hacking and credit-card fraud as he had 200 stolen credit-card numbers. Although he wasn't charged with hacking Miley's email account, he was charged for a MySpace spamming scheme he ran, which earned him more than $100,000. He was sentenced to three years' probation.

DID YOU KNOW?

Hackers targeted Miley a year later, too. They hacked into her YouTube account and posted a video saying she'd died. Thankfully, her friend Mandy posted up a message to say it was all lies and that Miley was absolutely fine.

CHAPTER FOUR

FAMILY COMES FIRST

Miley is extremely close to all of her family but the person she was closest to was her 'Pappy', who died in 2006. Pappy was Miley's granddad – her dad's dad – and she misses him every single day. When he died, she set up The Pappy Cyrus Foundation in his memory, to raise money for children who need help in America.

She talked to *MediaBlvd Magazine* about how she felt in April 2009:

This is the third year since my granddad died. That was a hard day because he was like my best friend, so I have a foundation called The Pappy Cyrus Foundation. We're working with all kinds of different people. We actually did a couple of trips back and forth to the

White House. One of the reasons I was at the inauguration was so that we could get all of America involved. It's something that's so important. We deal with homeless shelters.

When I was on tour in 2007, my best friend died of cystic fibrosis, right after my granddad had died, so I just had a hard time with cancers and that kind of stuff. That's mostly who I work with. Then I did a tour with the Jonas Brothers and we ended up raising $2.5 million for City of Hope, which went to cures and studies for kids. It was really amazing to watch the process. We got to go to the hospitals and watch them do all these crazy things. We were sitting there watching live cells being placed and it was amazing. That was one of the coolest experiences.

Miley will never forget Pappy and the lessons that he taught her. He inspired her so much. Visiting him when she knew he was dying was really hard and she wrote the song 'I Miss You' for him just before he died.

DID YOU KNOW?

When Miley was a child, her granddad bought her a real live donkey for a present. She was so happy and she named him Eeyore. Her granddad told her that Eeyore was half-zebra because he had white ankles. He was only joking but Miley believed him.

In December 2009 Miley got her first tattoo, 'Just Breathe', on her rib cage in memory of her friend Vanessa and of her granddad. She told *Harper's Bazaar*, 'It reminds me not to take things for granted. I mean breathing – that was something none of them could do, the most basic thing. And I put it near my heart, because that is where they will always be.'

Initially, fans were shocked when she got her first tattoo because she had vowed in 2008 that she would never get one because of her fear of needles. Miley said this because she was working on *Hannah Montana* and was trying to live up to Disney's expectations of her. She was lying because she was always going to have tattoos as soon as she was old enough.

Miley's parents always provided a loving home for her and her siblings but their relationship hasn't always been solid and on 26 October 2010 Billy Ray filed for divorce from Miley's mum Tish, citing 'irreconcilable differences'. The next day they released a joint statement to US magazine *People*. They said, 'As you can imagine, this is a very difficult time for our family. We are trying to work through some personal matters. We appreciate your thoughts and prayers.'

When Billy Ray was interviewed on *The View* on 18 March 2011, he revealed that he and Tish were no longer getting a divorce. Miley's fans were thrilled that her parents were working to save their marriage.

Sadly, two years later, on 13 June 2013, Tish filed for divorce from Billy Ray, 'irreconcilable differences' once again being cited. Miley seemed to side with her mum, tweeting angrily that Billy Ray needed to 'tell the truth'. She wrote, '@billyraycyrus since you won't reply to my texts I'm giving you an hour to tell the truth or ill tell it for you.'

She also posted up a photo of herself with another woman

but this was soon deleted. Four minutes after her post she tweeted, 'Wtf? My twitter was just actin all types of cray!'

The following month Tish and Billy Ray went to couples' therapy. Having been married for 22 years, they were going to work to save their marriage. They went on dates together, with Tish posting up a picture of the two of them on Instagram, showing fans that they were back in love with each other.

Watching her parents work at their marriage has taught Miley a lot and, when asked by *Rolling Stone* magazine about relationships, she replied, 'It's all back-and-forth. Like, when my parents are good, they're good, and when they're not, they're not, but they always get themselves back on track. They never put pressure on themselves. And I think that's a better way to be. That's how they've gotten themselves through everything they've been through. The best thing my parents ever taught me is that you don't have to be attached at the f****** hip. You don't have to be holding hands all the f****** time. Like my dad can go chill in Nashville for a while, and my mom can stay in LA, but they're still walking side by side. And as long as you're on the same path, one can go a little ahead, and one can be a little behind.'

Miley and her mum are super-close and, when Miley was filming *Hannah Montana*, Tish would go to work with her daughter every day to make sure that she was happy and safe. She always insisted that Miley maintained as normal a teenage life as possible and she wouldn't let her work too hard. When Miley splits up from boyfriends, it is Tish who supports her through it.

Tish is Miley's rock and she's always there for her daughter whenever she needs help or advice. Her love for cheerleading was what got Miley into cheerleading in the first place and gave her the inner confidence to go for auditions.

Tish did so well raising Miley and her brothers and sisters when Billy Ray was on the road and couldn't be with her. She is a real inspiration to Miley. Sometimes she can be a bit annoying though, like any mum. When Miley was still living at home, Tish would ground her when she misbehaved and punish her by confiscating some of her things, as Miley explained to tribute.ca in 2007: 'My mom can be pretty strict sometimes. I do get grounded, all the time! She took away my phone, my computer privileges, TV (although I don't watch a lot of TV so that one was OK), but mostly the computer and the phone are the first to go!'

DID YOU KNOW?

When she was younger, Miley used to become very upset when she wasn't sure what to wear. She felt under pressure to look good all the time.

Miley and her mum are so close that sometimes they fight like cat and dog but they always make up. They are like sisters, rather than mother and daughter really. When Miley was fourteen, they would go out and children would think that her mum was Hannah Montana because she had long blonde hair, whereas Miley had naturally brown hair.

One of the things that Miley is always conscious of is the need to make her parents proud of her. 'The last thing I ever want to do is disappoint my parents. My mom's dad died when she was eighteen, and if something ever happened to one of my parents, I'd want them to go knowing I made them proud,' she told *Glamour* in April 2009. 'I think it's selfish to go out partying all the time, especially if you have little ones [in your family]. I have a nine-year-old sister, and I don't want her to go to school and have people make fun of her for it.'

As well as being close to her mum, Miley is extremely close to her 'Mammie' – her maternal grandma. She thinks she is a lot like her Mammie as she is very loyal. When she was younger and started going out, her Mammie would tell her to put some more blusher on. Miley's grandma loves make-up and always wears it.

Miley might be a multi-millionaire but it is time that is most precious to her. She so rarely has any spare time to do her own thing that, when she gets the chance, she likes to try a new hobby or visit the people she loves the most. Sometimes she cancels interviews and appearances if she is emotionally drained because she could make herself ill; sometimes she just needs Miley time.

DID YOU KNOW?

When Miley is running late, she doesn't rush; she just takes her time. She can't get stressed because of her heart condition.

Miley has never been spoiled by her family and having five siblings has helped her stay grounded. She has one half-sister, two half-brothers, a younger brother and a younger sister.

Miley's oldest sibling is Brandi, her half-sister. She is Tish's biological daughter and was adopted by Billy Ray when she was a young child. Brandi is six years older than Miley so had moved out into her own place while Miley was still filming *Hannah Montana*. Even though they didn't live together, they stayed very close, with Brandi taking Miley on shopping trips and out for meals in their favourite restaurants. Brandi has always been someone that Miley can confide in.

Brandi has done a bit of acting alongside Miley and on her own too. She has been in *The Real Miley Cyrus*, *Billy Ray Cyrus: Home at Last*, an episode of *Hannah Montana* and *Zoey 101*. Brandi's real passion is music and she's in a band called Frank + Derol. She is the guitarist and also writes their songs; Brandi, Codi and Megan are looking for a record deal and are performing as much as they can in the meantime. Brandi has lots of confidence on stage because she played the guitar for Miley when she was touring and also on *Hannah Montana*.

Brandi's Twitter account is @BrandiCyrus and in her bio she describes herself as 'songwriter, musician, blogger, designer, competitive equestrian. I have faith in a Savior who gives me LIFE.' Her personality is very different to Miley's, as she explained to E! online: 'She's definitely louder and she has a very big personality. She likes to be the center of attention and entertain everyone and I'm much more low-key. Attention makes me nervous.'

She agreed that Miley and Noah are very similar but that they enjoy different things. She explained, '[Noah] enjoy[s] normal things a little more than Miley... like riding horses.

[Miley doesn't have the] attention span. She's like, "Nope. Boring. No."'

Miley admitted herself that she doesn't like horse riding, telling Josh Eells from *Rolling Stone*,

> I love animals, but I don't really like riding animals. Like, I don't love being on a horse – it's just not my thing. I feel kinda bad. Like, I just want to pet you. I don't really want to put you to work. But cats – cats are f****** creepy... Every time I see a cat, I think it's gonna turn on me. It's gonna turn for the worst. I don't ever see loyalty in cats. They're gonna scratch you, and then run away. Same with little dogs. Did you know Yorkies were bred to kill mice in the Queen's palace? I had a Yorkshire Terrier, and if I was a rat, it definitely would have eaten me. And Chihuahuas are the most scary animals on the planet. I'm terrified of Chihuahuas.

Trace is Miley's oldest half-brother and Brandi's full brother. Four years older than Miley, he is Tish's biological son and was adopted by Billy Ray when he was small. His biological father is a drummer called Baxter Neal Helson. Trace was sixteen when they moved to Los Angeles from Tennessee. Obsessed with music, he has been in several bands. He was in a band called Metro Station with his band mate Mason Musso (who is the brother of Mitchel Musso, who played Oliver in *Hannah Montana*). Once they disbanded in early 2010, he became known as Ashland HIGH and released solo albums.

DID YOU KNOW?

People used to think that the sibling Miley was most like was her little sister Noah but she always insisted her personality was more like Trace's.

Trace's Twitter account is @TraceCyrus and his website address is www.smhpclothing.com. He is passionate about art and his whole body is covered in tattoos. Tish took him for his first tattoo the day after he turned eighteen and he has been getting more and more tattoos ever since. His tattoo artist thinks his whole head will be covered in tattoos one day. Trace's tattoos include: Ashland on his face, lots of tattoos showing his Christian faith, cowboy boots, a grenade, two 'Mom' tattoos, 'Tennessee' and 'Hollywood' on his knuckles, a gorgeous brown-haired girl on one arm and a zombie version of the same girl on the other arm... and many more. Underneath his right eye he has a cross and below his left eye he has two feathers, which represent his close relationship to Billy Ray.

When Trace isn't performing, he concentrates on his own clothing line – Southern Made Hollywood Paid. On his website he writes, 'I've always been into fashion and thought it would be amazing to have a clothing line – just never thought I would have a chance to do something like that.

'Once I finally had the opportunity to have one of my own I really wanted the name of it to represent me. That is why I decided on Southern Made Hollywood Paid. I feel it tells a lot about me, my life, and my story. I love any way to express myself in life, and that's why I started SMHP.'

In an interview with Lehigh Valley Music in April 2013 Trace was asked how much contact he has with Miley. He replied,

I see Miley and my family every chance I get, but you have to understand. Me and my family, we're one of the busiest families in the music business, I feel like. My dad's always doing something, I'm always doing something, Miley's always doing something. So the time we do spend together, I feel like we really treasure it and we make the best out of that time. But it's definitely not as much as I would like. But in the future, all of our careers are going to slow down, so we're just trying to live in this moment as much as we can and make the careers as much as we can.

But I live five miles from Miley and my parents, so we definitely still see each other whenever we want, you know? But like I said, it's hard to get our schedules to work out with each other's.

Christopher Cody is Miley's half-brother. He was born in April 1992. Christopher and Miley have met a few times but he was brought up in South Carolina, over 2,000 miles away from Miley's home in Los Angeles.

Christopher has managed to live life out of the limelight, thanks to his mum Kristen. While Miley worked on *Hannah Montana*, he worked in an electronics store for $7.50 (about £5) an hour. He rarely speaks about Miley and Billy Ray but he did do a rare interview with the *Mirror* in 2009.

Christopher told the journalist, 'She [Miley] doesn't play

the superstar in private. She's a normal teenager having fun and she can laugh at herself. She's the same now as she was before all this fame. She's still my goofy sister. Miley is not a self-obsessed person at all.'

He showed the journalists texts that he had received from Billy Ray. On Christmas Day he had texted his dad 'Merry Christmas' but Billy Ray hadn't replied until 4 January, when he sent a message saying, 'Hey bud, where you been? You disappeared on us.' Christopher had sent him one back, saying, 'I disappeared? You disappeared. I tried to get a hold of you.'

Miley's little brother is called Braison and he is two years younger than her. By the time he was a teenager he was a lot taller than her. They have very different personalities, as Miley explained in a tweet in July 2009. She posted two pictures of them standing next to each other and wrote, 'How ironic. My brother is wearing all black and I am wearing all white. Story of our life together. Brothers and sisters are as similar as hands and feet.'

Like most little brothers, Braison enjoys winding Miley up and once, when she asked him if he'd be in a band with her, he turned her down, saying he was too good for her.

Braison has done a bit of acting himself. Like Miley, he was in an episode of *Doc* and he appeared in an episode of *Hannah Montana*, back in 2008. But acting isn't his passion and he prefers playing basketball. He likes playing one on one and putting Billy Ray through his paces but missed being able to play basketball with his dad when Billy Ray was one of the contestants on *Dancing with the Stars* in 2007. Braison, Miley and the rest of the Cyrus family loved going to the studio to cheer him on but he wasn't the best dancer by a long shot. Still, he managed to finish in fifth place, which was a good achievement.

Like the rest of the Cyrus family, Braison is into his music and formed a band while he was still at school called Lazy Randy with his friends Josh Reaves and Lashette Showers. His late-night playing used to really get on Miley's nerves, especially if she had a busy filming schedule the next day, because Braison's bedroom was only two rooms away from hers. She explained to the host of American TV show *The View* in March 2009, 'He just got a drum set. It's torture. I hate it.'

After he graduated from school Braison enrolled at the Pasadena School of the Arts but also played in another band, Friends of the Family. When he was eighteen, he signed for Wilhelmina Models, which has Kendall and Kylie Jenner on its books, as well as many other top models. His first modelling job was on a spread for *Troix* magazine, titled 'Boys of Summer'. He gave a short Q&A too, confessing that he has a crush on Katy Perry and that he wants to be an actor. When Miley learned that Braison was going to be a model, she found it funny and tweeted a black and white image of him next to a black and white image of herself with the words, 'Woahhhhhh! Who's prettier? I'm voting Braison? Haha @tyrabanks who do YOU think is ANTM?! ;)' (ANTM is an abbreviation for Tyra's show *America's Next Top Model*.)

Braison's Twitter account is @BraisonCyrus and his website for his music is braisoncyrus.bandcamp.com. On his website you can download his original tracks, 'Just 1 Touch' and 'Disappear'.

In July 2012 the Cyrus family had a fright when Braison was rushed to hospital with heavy bleeding in his mouth. He had to hold a jug to catch the blood that was pouring out of him; the flow was so heavy, it was choking him. Doctors realised he was haemorrhaging and he was rushed into theatre. Naturally, Tish and Billy Ray were extremely worried about him and he could have bled to death if the doctors hadn't acted quickly.

After undergoing surgery the bleeding stopped and Braison was allowed home the next day. He tweeted, 'Thank you everyone for the twitter love. Ive made a full recovery. Y'all are good folks. Thanks for giving a damn. I got my tonsils out last week. Not sure what happened exactly but long story short my artery opened and I was bleeding a lot. All good now. Thanks to good doctors.'

The youngest member of the Cyrus clan is Miley's little sister Noah. She is seven years younger than Miley and loves cheerleading and acting. Her biggest love, however, is horse riding and she has a horse called Constantine and a pony called Comet. Noah's big ambition is to represent the US at the Olympics and afterwards maybe become a horse trainer.

DID YOU KNOW?

For her thirteenth birthday Noah decided to try to raise funds for the campaign against the use of horse-drawn carriages in New York. She asked her friends to donate $13 to her favourite charity NYCLASS (New Yorkers for Livable and Safe Streets). She also held a party at the Level 3 nightclub in Hollywood and posed for some fun photos with Miley and a cutout of Harry Styles from One Direction.

Noah is very clever and used to confuse Miley with some of the words she came out with when she was really small. Billy Ray and Tish wanted to protect their girls' innocence for as long as possible so, when Miley and Noah were growing up, they only had 10 TV channels they could watch, rather than the thousands of channels available on cable. Because of this, Noah and Miley missed out on watching gossip and reality shows but they didn't really mind because it meant they spent more quality time together as a family.

They also avoided reading gossip magazines and looking at what people were writing about them online. Miley explained to *Rolling Stone*,

My parents have never allowed tabloids in the house. When my mom used to have assistants or whatever and they would bring tabloids over, she would be like, 'Can't work with us. I don't want my kids reading that.' So my dad doesn't really know what they're saying about me or our family – which is better. It's good that he doesn't know how to Google and all that s***. My dad barely knows how to use the computer. It literally takes him 45 minutes to send a tweet. He's like, 'Can I do a picture on my BlackBerry? Is there an app for that?' I'm like, 'Dad, you don't have an iPhone. You don't even know what that means.'

In another interview with *Viva Press* Miley explained what it was like, growing up with her parents. She revealed,

I barely ever heard my mom cuss. My mom is the sweetest lady ever. She spells the word crap. My mom is so sweet. That was her thing that she really hated. Like when you first start hearing cuss words and you start saying them – I remember like one time I think I called my sister a bitch for the first time. I was done. I was locked in my room, my mouth washed out with soap, everything. I was like, 'Mom she is. That's what she is. She's a bitch.' I was like in so much trouble. I'll never forget the first time I did that. I got in so much trouble. That was kind of the thing that my mom was like really mad about. My dad, I think he probably wouldn't say it but he might have thought it was a little funny. Like a little kid hearing it and then saying it. That was like the one thing that my mom – and my mom is really weird with TV.

My dad would always let us watch *The Simpsons*. We would stay up all night watching Cartoon Network with my dad and she hated it. She just thought everything – even *Tom & Jerry* – was too violent. My mom hated it. My dad would always let us watch any cartoon that we wanted. My mom was really weird with TV. We didn't really watch a lot of TV. She's like, 'I don't want to see the commercials. I don't want you guys being sold on everything like so young.' If you watch Nickelodeon or whatever there is like all the commercials for every kind of game and dolls. She just didn't really want it.

Noah is the member of the Cyrus family who has had the most 'normal' life but she is used to the paparazzi following her around when she is with her parents or Miley. She has acted in quite a few films and TV shows but she isn't as passionate about acting as her siblings. Noah played Gracie Herbert in *Doc*, a trick-or-treater in *Mostly Ghostly*, numerous girls in *Hannah Montana* and in TV series *Take 2* she played Allison, Adamley and Deb. She provided her voice in the 2008 animated movie *Ponyo* and in the TV series *The Emperor's New School*.

DID YOU KNOW?

Frankie Jonas was also in *Ponyo*. The younger brother of the Jonas Brothers, he did several TV interviews alongside Noah and they got on really well. They sang the movie's theme tune together.

Noah loves having a famous sister and the different privileges it brings her. She loves popping over to Miley's house and taking a look through her closet and borrowing things, but there are some items that Miley won't let her borrow. Both girls are really into fashion and, when Noah has a special event to go to, Miley will help her do her make-up.

When Noah was younger, she had a huge crush on Justin Bieber and was able to meet him when Miley took her to an awards show in Canada. She has some of Justin's clothes as a memento from that day because his stylist let her take some home with her, all because she was Miley's sister.

When Miley first got a 'buzz cut', Noah told the media that she would never cut her hair like Miley's but she quickly changed her mind. On 6 November 2013 her big sister

Brandi posted a photo of them both on Instagram, showing Noah with a buzz cut on one side of her head and herself standing behind her thirteen-year-old sister, looking shocked. She wrote, 'Lil sis @noahcyrus just one up'd me.'

CHAPTER FIVE

BEST OF
BOTH WORLDS

Miley's first tour kicked off on 18 October 2007 and finished on 3 January 2008. It was called the Best of Both Worlds Tour and was a sell-out. Miley loved every single performance – having the opportunity to perform in front of thousands of people every night was a dream come true. When she is on stage, Miley is at her happiest and it makes her feel alive.

Travelling to each concert venue drives most performers mad because they get bored and frustrated but fourteen-year-old Miley took it all in her stride. She loved her tour bus, which her mom had designed to be just like their home in California. She didn't get homesick because she travelled with her family, who wanted to support her every step of the way. Miley admits that the two downsides to the tour were the food – because it just wasn't the same as her mom's cooking – and having to perform the same songs again and again, every night, in the same order. She would have preferred it if she'd been able to change things around a bit but this wasn't an option; she had to do as she was told.

DID YOU KNOW?

While they were travelling on Miley's tour bus, her brothers and sisters used Miley's toothbrush to brush their hair and eyebrows – just to wind her up.

Whenever the tour bus parked up at a new venue, Miley would rush inside and head for a shower. The bathroom on her tour bus was really small and often she couldn't use the shower because Trace and Braison had used up all the hot water. Her dad didn't stay over on the bus as he liked going home each night and looking after the family's pets but he still went to as many concerts as he could.

When one of Miley's fans asked her if she ever gets nervous singing in front of thousands of people at her Hannah Montana concerts, she replied, 'Really, now it's like second nature. I know my body is ready to perform at certain times. My mom was laughing the other day when I didn't have a show. At five o'clock, when I usually would be warming up, I was super-hyper. She's, like, "You're just so used to being ready to go at five."'

Miley was criticised in the press when a Hannah Montana double was used during her show. Her PR company issued the following statement to explain why this happened:

To help speed the transition from Hannah to Miley, there is a production element during the performance of 'We Got the Party' incorporating a body double for Miley.

After Hannah has completed the featured verse on the duet with the Jonas Brothers, a body double appears approximately one to two minutes prior to the end of the song in order to allow Miley to remove the Hannah wig and costume and transform into Miley for her solo set. Other than during this very brief transitional moment in the show, Miley performs live during the entirety of both the Hannah and Miley segments of the concert.

Miley was asked about the body double during an interview with *USA Today* shortly after the reports came out. She said, 'We don't even do it anymore because we changed songs. But it wasn't for the reason everyone was saying – because I'm not singing, because I'm not this, because I'm not that. It was a total technical thing. When I'm shooting *Hannah Montana*, it takes me an hour and a half to go from Hannah to Miley. [On stage], I have a minute, fifty seconds. There's no way; I need a good three to four minutes. So I did have to take a double to dance for that minute.'

While Miley was on tour, an animated film she had worked on was released. Disney's *Bolt* came out on 21 November 2007. The film was a huge deal for Miley because in it she was playing the main human character. She had lots of lines to learn but because she was only providing Penny's voice she could have a script in front of her, which must have helped.

The film's plot centres around the friendship of Penny and a dog called Bolt, played by John Travolta. Penny is a twelve-year-old child actress who acts alongside Bolt the dog in a TV show called *Bolt*. She loves him and he helps her deal with being a star. When Bolt goes missing, she is devastated but the people at the studio don't care, simply replacing Bolt with another white dog. Bolt makes new furry friends and manages to make it back to Penny. There is a fire and Bolt saves the day. The film concludes when Penny realises that she doesn't want to be in the show anymore and moves to the country with Bolt.

Miley really enjoyed recording *Bolt* and felt that children could learn a lot from watching the film. She explained to *Teen Hollywood*, 'I love all my dogs and I hope that, after seeing this film, people will want to go home and love their dog. I hope kids realise, one, that you love your pets and know what great friends they can be. And two, that no matter what you do for a living, you have to realise that that can go away in a second.'

As well as voicing Penny for the film, Miley also recorded *Bolt*'s theme song, 'I Thought I Lost You', with John Travolta. A feel-good track, it earned her an MTV Award for Best Song from a Movie. It was also nominated for a Golden Globe and a Critics Choice Award.

DID YOU KNOW?

Miley might have been a nickname that Billy Ray and Tish came up with but since she became famous it has become a popular baby name. In 2008 it was the 128th most popular girl's name in America. Miley explained

---

to the *Sun* in November 2008 that she wishes her name had stayed unique. She said, 'In a lot of ways it is an honour for your name to be put into all those kinds of things, but then again it's kind of sad. I like being one of the only ones. I have just moved into a new neighbourhood and the girl just three doors down from me is called Miley too. It's spelt differently though. I was so disappointed.'

Two days after *Bolt* was released Miley turned fifteen. She loves her birthdays and all she wanted was to be able to go back to Nashville and eat her grandma's cake. She just wanted a day to chill out with her family close by but this couldn't happen because she had shows to do.

Even though she couldn't get her wish, her family still wanted her to enjoy her birthday so they threw her a surprise party. They all dressed up in silly costumes from the 1980s and Billy Ray wore an awful blond mullet wig as he hosted the night. He'd arranged for all of Miley's friends from Nashville to be there. It was a big surprise for Miley because he was supposed to be on the other side of the USA so she wasn't expecting to see him on her birthday.

After she had performed her birthday concert Miley received a surprise gift. She revealed to Office Max, 'The whole crew – and we have like 13 semi-trucks travelling with us for the tour – the whole crew came on stage and they gave me a beautiful watch as a present that I'll always remember.'

To make it up to fans who hadn't been able to get tickets

for one of her Best of Both Worlds concerts Miley decided to make *Hannah Montana & Miley Cyrus: Best of Both Worlds Concert 3D*, a film of the concert. Fans could go and watch it in their local cinemas (and later buy it on DVD). She divulged to the *Baltimore Sun*, 'It was kind of like a 3D reality show. It was wild, having them follow you around with their cameras and, you know, me and someone would get in an argument or something bad would happen, and they would run up and be like, "Can I mike you?" And it's like, "Aw, come on."'

Miley was really passionate about doing the concert in 3D for the fans who couldn't be there, as she explained to the *Associated Press* when it was released:

[We did it] mostly because of the tickets and there were so many people that didn't get to come to the show. This is like better than front row. You could reach out and feel like you could touch my hand, you could see me right then, right there, right in front of you, which is so fun. Also just to be able to see behind the scenes, which I think is the [cleverest] part of anything. Just getting to see what goes into this. They can walk around knowing what real hard work it is. I mean, I think I have the easiest job.

Miley felt ill during one of her Best of Both Worlds performances and had to be checked out by doctors. They discovered that she had a hole in her heart and diagnosed her with a heart condition called tachycardia. People with tachycardia have heart rates that exceed the normal range for a resting heartbeat. It means that their hearts are pumping faster so blood is pumped less efficiently, which means that their bodies receive less blood than they need. This can make the person feel ill and struggle to breathe if they exert themselves too much. Because Miley has this condition, she has to be careful that she doesn't overheat when she's performing and that she doesn't push herself too hard.

During an interview with *Xposé* Miley advised an interviewer with tachycardia on how to deal with stress. She said, 'I always just try to think, step away from the situation and put [myself] ten years from where [I am] now and then say, "All right, is this really going to be significant in my life? Is this going to change where I'm going to be in ten years? At my happiest moment is this going to be weighing on my mind... no." Otherwise I'll just OCD myself to death. I'll be like I have to call, I have to fix dinner... finally, it's like, it'll all work out.'

Miley released a live album on 11 March 2008 entitled *Best of Both Worlds Concert*. It was number 3 in the USA and Canada, number 6 in Belgium and number 10 in Ireland. However, it only managed to reach number 29 in the UK charts.

Track Listing:
1. Rock Star
2. Life's What You Make It
3. Just Like You
4. Nobody's Perfect
5. Pumpin' Up the Party

6. I Got Nerve
7. We Got the Party
8. Start All Over
9. Good and Broken
10. See You Again
11. Let's Dance
12. East Northumberland High
13. G.N.O (Girls Night Out)
14. The Best of Both Worlds

Miley's fourth album was released on 22 July 2008. *Breakout* was her first independent album away from Hannah Montana. She co-wrote eight of the songs on the album and it was a huge success. It was number 1 in America, Australia and Canada, number 2 in New Zealand, number 6 in Italy and number 10 in the UK and Japan. To Miley it was proof that she had fans in her own right.

Her favourite track from the album was 'Fly on the Wall'. Miley loved the 'Fly on the Wall' video because her mom was the one who edited it with her. She knew that if she wanted some control over the video, and for it to show the real Miley, she needed her mom to step in and take control. Tish did a great job, with the help of the video's producers Antonina Armato and Tim James, of course.

Miley also liked the overall concept of the video, as she explained to *Access Hollywood*: 'The concept is kind of *Thriller*-esque [sic]. It's kind of like where the paparazzi become these zombies and they're all like attacking me. And my boyfriend is trying to save me, but I don't know if he's a paparazzo too. So, it's like me trying to hide and get away. It's really fun, but I'm escaping from my boyfriend and escaping from the paparazzi and trying to find my way through the whole video.'

Track Listing:
1. Breakout
2. 7 Things
3. The Driveway
4. Girls Just Wanna Have Fun
5. Full Circle
6. Fly on the Wall
7. Bottom of the Ocean
8. Wake Up America
9. These Four Walls
10. Simple Song
11. Goodbye
12. See You Again

Miley was so glad she wasn't on tour for her sixteenth birthday. She was determined to have a party like no other and wanted as many Smilers as possible to come along. Her party was held at Disneyland and thousands of people came to help her celebrate, including, to Miley's delight, her best friend Lesley. The event raised thousands of dollars for charity.

Before her party started Miley told *GMA:* 'This is gonna be I think like the craziest sweet sixteen ever because there's like seven thousand people coming, there's seven thousand cupcakes that go out to everyone. I'm like, I don't want to be the person baking the cupcakes because that's going to take a while!'

There was a parade with Miley dressed like a princess, and a whole host of other celebrities and Disney characters joined in too. She performed as well because, even though it was her birthday, she felt like she should give something back to her fans. It was a great night and one that Miley will, no doubt, never forget.

As well as getting to have her party at Disneyland, Miley got some great presents. Her dad treated her to her own recording studio and her mum bought her a puppy called Sofie. Miley told *TV Guide*, 'I got a dog today, so I couldn't be happier. A little doggie named Sofie. I started crying my eyes off, I was so dorky but I couldn't help it.'

Because Miley's birthday party at Disney was held a month before her actual birthday her friends decided that on the night of her birthday they would throw her a party. It was the night of the American Music Awards so afterwards Taylor Swift and Ashley Tisdale presented her with a huge cake. Taylor told *Star* magazine, 'Us girls got together and thought it would be fun to do a little surprise party for Miley; she deserves it.'

DID YOU KNOW?

During the filming of the third and fourth seasons of *Hannah Montana* Miley was so busy that she had hardly any time to go outdoors in the sunshine. She confessed to *Harper's Bazaar*, 'I had to have [the producers] put sun lamps inside because I was getting depressed from a lack of vitamin D.'

CHAPTER SIX

DISAPPOINTING DISNEY

When Miley posed for the front cover of *Vanity Fair* back in April 2008, she had no idea the trouble it would cause. The second the magazine hit newsstands the media went crazy, saying the image of Miley wrapped in a bed sheet, revealing her bare back, wasn't appropriate. Parent groups called for *Hannah Montana* to be axed because in their eyes Miley was no longer a good role model. Their cruel words really hurt Miley and her family at the time. In the days that followed the magazine's publication three statements were released: one from Disney, one from Miley and one from *Vanity Fair*.

The Disney statement read, 'Unfortunately, as the article suggests, a situation was created to deliberately manipulate a fifteen-year-old in order to sell magazines.'

Miley's statement added, 'I took part in a photo shoot that was supposed to be "artistic" and now, seeing the photographs and reading the story, I feel so embarrassed. I never intended for any of this to happen and I apologize to my fans who I care so deeply about.'

Vanity Fair obviously wasn't happy with getting the blame and a spokesperson for the magazine said, 'Miley's parents and/or minders were on the set all day. Since the photo was taken digitally, they saw it on the shoot and everyone thought it was a beautiful and natural portrait of Miley.'

Two years after the event Miley told *Harper's Bazaar* how she really felt at the time. She confessed, 'Here, my parents are thinking they're seeing a beautiful picture by a major photographer, and the people of America want to see something dirty in that? It doesn't make sense to us because [my family] doesn't look for negativity. But people don't want to say "What a great performance" or "What a great shot". No one wants to look at something like that and see the positive because it doesn't sell a magazine.'

Thankfully, Miley got to escape the media glare after the *Vanity Fair* scandal as she had to be on the set of her new film *Hannah Montana: The Movie*. Filming started in the spring of 2008 but it wasn't to be released worldwide until 10 April 2009. Just before the premiere of *Hannah Montana: The Movie* she tweeted, 'Getting ready for the red carpet! This is my VERY 1st film I can't believe it's finally here! Thank u! & mommy thank U 4 allowing me 2 dream!' The film was a huge success right from the word go and was number 1 in the box-office chart on its opening weekend, making a massive $34 million in ticket sales! Its premiere in Nashville drew huge crowds as fans waited for hours for the opportunity to see Miley, who was joined by her dad, her close friend Taylor Swift and many more stars from the film. Miley and Billy Ray were glad that *Hannah Montana: The Movie* was filmed in their home state of Tennessee. Originally, film bosses had been planning on shooting it elsewhere but she and her father were so passionate about it being filmed in Tennessee that Billy Ray set it upon himself to convince them that Tennessee would be the perfect location. He left Los Angeles, flew back home and took as many photos of potential filming locations as possible. The producers were so impressed with what Billy Ray showed them that they changed their minds and the Cyrus stars got their way. This really boosted the Tennessee film industry and created a lot of jobs for people in the area. Miley told *CNN*, '[Filming the movie] actually gave me time to relax, and it was when my career was just starting to take off... when I was just starting to travel. It was at a time when I needed to go back home and it couldn't have been more of a perfect time.' This mirrored what happens to Miley Stewart in the film. She is forced to go back home and has to decide what she really wants: to be famous or to be a normal girl. Billy Ray explained to a reporter, 'This is definitely an example of art imitating life imitating art... It's so important to be aware of where you're at and be focused on where you're going but, more importantly, never forget where you came from. You can't fake going home. That was her home.'

For the film, Miley had to develop her acting skills as the director had high expectations. Peter Chelsom wanted to teach Miley how to improve her focus and concentration in scenes. He explained to online entertainment news agency BANG Showbiz, 'We did stuff before we started filming that was just the kind of stuff you'd do at drama school, you know. Did I give her a detention? No. I made her read a sonnet though. A Shakespeare sonnet. She said, "Oh no, I can't." I said, "Let's do it because it'll be the most difficult thing you'll ever do." We did all that kind of stuff. It was remarkable.

'We used to have this code where I would say, "This means focus, because I don't want to have to shout at you across the set!"'

When Miley had to kiss Lucas Till in *Hannah Montana: The Movie*, it might have been hard for her boyfriend at the time, Justin Gaston, to watch but she didn't have a problem with it.

She told reporters, 'He's seen the movie, and it's only acting, so I guess you have got to keep that in your mind. And I'm sure it's probably a little hard, but we're actors. We have got to be good at our jobs.'

Lucas was really happy that he got to work with Miley and he told *CNN*, 'She's really nice and really [endearing], and she really cares about people. She's a good friend, very loyal.' He also hinted that 'there was a lot more there to that kiss than you see'. When Miley was asked whether Lucas was a good kisser, she replied, 'Meh, he's OK. No, I'm just kidding. I don't know. I think I was too busy thinking about my next line to think about it.'

Both Miley and Billy Ray were really happy with the way *Hannah Montana: The Movie* turned out. They were able to show even more of their deep bond, as Miley's dad explained to the *San Francisco Chronicle*:

> The movie itself is as close to real life as it can be, while still keeping the comedy and the whole stuff that makes the *Hannah Montana* series work. Even down to the song I sing, 'Back to Tennessee'. That becomes the theme of the movie and the cornerstone of the film. The words and lyrics are about living there and knowing we both had to go home. My dad had this saying: 'Always look toward the future, but most importantly, never forget where you came from and who you are.' And that's what this movie and the song are about.

DID YOU KNOW?

After filming finished, Miley kidnapped the chickens that were used in the movie because she wanted to give them a better life on her Tennessee farm. She sneaked on set and whisked them away before anyone could stop her. Animal charity PETA was so impressed that it gave her a Compassionate Citizen Award. PETA assistant director Dan Shannon told the press, 'Miley's heart is as big as her smile. We hope that her act of compassion will inspire her fans to be kind to animals too.'

When *Hannah Montana: The Movie* topped the box office, it made Miley want to do more movies, but away from *Hannah Montana*. She wanted edgier roles; to play characters that her fans wouldn't expect from her. Also, she wanted to record more music but wasn't sure which direction to go in. When MTV asked her about recording country songs, she replied, 'Maybe one day... I'll leave that to the pros, but I don't know what I want to do.'

While they were filming *Hannah Montana: The Movie*, Miley and her co-star Emily Osment bonded. Emily played Miley's best friend, Lilly Truscott, in the show and when they had started working together the two girls didn't get on. During the first and second seasons of *Hannah Montana* they would fight and argue when the cameras weren't rolling. After filming the movie their relationship improved, which made filming the third season of the show much easier.

Miley didn't like having to pretend that she and Emily were best friends in real life but it was something she had to do when they were promoting *Hannah Montana* in the early days.

In a 2008 interview with *Teen Mag* Miley said, 'When we first met, automatically she and I were really, really close. When we're together we're never quiet because there's so much to talk about and there are so many stories. Every day it's something new for us. When you're with someone all the time, it's more than just she and I are friends, we're sisters now. When we first met we had an instant friendship and now we're more like sisters. We love each other like sisters. We fight like sisters. It's always like that.'

Miley didn't like having to lie but she was forced to do so in order to give the public the impression that everything was good between them. In 2012 she was interviewed on *The Conversation* and was able to share how it felt to be her back then. She said,

I feel I was so trained in my interviews to be All-American or whatever. I just got so set in the way of saying the same things I did when I was twelve years old.

I had to smile so much and I had to say so much of the same thing. I finally had to look inside and say, 'What do I really think about this? Do I really think that or am I just trained to say that? Or have I said it for so many years now that that's what people expect me to say, so now I say it so I don't have to say something else and be creative?'

I guess I kind of realised that my whole life isn't one giant press junket. I don't have to be smiling all the time and always have the perfect answer.

Disney decided to release three albums in 2009, as well as *Hannah Montana: The Movie*, so Miley had a ridiculous amount of things to promote. The third season of *Hannah Montana* was still airing so she had to promote that too... a lot to ask of a sixteen-year-old girl.

Miley's first album of the year was a soundtrack to *Hannah Montana: The Movie*, which was released on 23 March 2009. It reached number 1 in the USA, Austria, Canada and New Zealand, number 2 in Norway and number 3 in the UK.

Track Listing:
1. You'll Always Find Your Way Back Home
2. Let's Get Crazy
3. The Good Life
4. Everything I Want
5. Don't Walk Away
6. Hoedown Throwdown
7. Dream
8. The Climb
9. Butterfly Fly Away
10. Backwards
11. Back to Tennessee
12. Crazier
13. Bless the Broken Road
14. Let's Do This
15. Spotlight
16. Game Over
17. What's Not to Like
18. The Best of Both Worlds: The 2009 Movie Mix

Four months later Miley's next album *Hannah Montana 3* was released on 2 July 2009. It performed slightly less well in the charts, reaching number 2 in the USA and Canada, number 4 in Austria and number 5 in the UK.

Track Listing:
1. It's All Right Here
2. Let's Do This
3. Mixed Up
4. He Could Be the One
5. Just a Girl
6. I Wanna Know You
7. Supergirl
8. Every Part of Me
9. Ice Cream Freeze (Let's Chill)
10. Don't Wanna Be Torn
11. Let's Get Crazy
12. I Wanna Know You
13. Let's Make This Last 4Ever
14. If We Were a Movie

Miley released an EP a month later on 28 August 2009. It was entitled *The Time of Our Lives* and was initially a Walmart exclusive before being released internationally.

Track Listing:
1. Kicking and Screaming
2. Party in the U.S.A.
3. When I Look at You
4. The Time of Our Lives
5. Talk Is Cheap
6. Obsessed
7. Before the Storm

Miley's track 'The Time of Our Lives' was written by Ke$ha,

who was just starting out as a songwriter. Later she would go on to be a huge pop star with tracks like 'Tik Tok' and 'We R Who We R'. Ke$ha was paid hardly anything for writing the song but she didn't mind because she loved working with Miley.

She confessed to *Seventeen* magazine, 'It was like $1.63 cents for a song I wrote – I think for Miley Cyrus. It was an embarrassingly tiny amount. But I never cashed it and it's on a bulletin board in my house.'

Miley was growing up and her taste in music was changing. She didn't just like pop; she listened to all types of music. And she liked artists that no one expected her to – artists such as Iron Maiden. When she started wearing an Iron Maiden T-shirt while out and about in Los Angeles people were really judgmental and said she was only wearing the top to pretend to be cool. But this couldn't have been further from the truth and Miley decided to set the record straight by releasing a homemade video on YouTube.

In it she said, 'I'm sure you all have seen me rocking an Iron Maiden shirt lately and I know there's been some people saying, "Oh, she's a poser," and, "The only reason she's wearing Iron Maiden is because she wants to be a rock star."

'So, Iron Maiden – "Run To The Hills", "Fear of the Dark", "Running Free", [all] good song[s], check it out. So thank you, guys. I actually do like Iron Maiden.'

She also started dating a guy called Justin Gaston. At twenty years old he was four years older than her so their relationship received some criticism in the press. Miley's parents didn't think the age gap was a problem; they really liked Justin and, him being a Christian, they thought he was a good influence on their daughter.

When they were dating, Miley announced on *The Rachael Ray Show*, 'I've never been closer to the Lord since I met him. He's really made me read my Bible. He's made me actually read the stories in the Bible – not the quick little verses – that not only help me, but show you how to help other people.'

Miley didn't fall head over heels in love with Justin straight away; in fact, she walked straight past him! It was Billy Ray who introduced her to Justin when they were on the *Hannah Montana* set. They became good friends first and then she realised how cute he was.

When the couple split after around a year together, Miley's fans were surprised because they'd seemed so happy together but Miley explained that she had to end it because having a long-distance relationship wasn't working out for them.

CHAPTER SEVEN
THE LAST SONG

In the summer break between filming *Hannah Montana* and touring, Miley filmed *The Last Song* in Australia. Filming started on 15 June 2009 and finished on 18 August 2009.

The Last Song is a film and a book written especially for Miley by award-winning writer Nicholas Sparks. He was contacted by the producer, Jennifer Gibgot, who asked if he had a script that would suit Miley and show off her acting skills. Nicholas didn't have anything suitable so he set about writing something and six weeks later he had developed *The Last Song*.

Nicholas insists, 'The finished product is definitely not a *Hannah Montana* movie. It's an ensemble piece with a talented cast that will appeal to audiences of all ages. Ronnie is a really compelling female character going through things that a lot of teenagers are going through. She's forced to really grow and mature through the course of the film.'

Miley thinks there are lots of similarities between herself and Ronnie. She told MTV, 'Mostly through the love of music. Mostly what she learns later is all about love and forgiveness and second chances – you know, in the career I'm in I have to do that a lot.

'There's no room for grudges and bitterness. She learns that later it's all about love and the people around you. And I think it's really beautifully done the way she has that transition and learns.'

When Nicholas set about writing the script, he was in touch with Miley and asked her to name her character. He must have trusted Miley a lot to ask her to do this. She chose the name Ronnie, after her pappy, who had been called Ron.

Playing the lead character in *The Last Song* was very challenging for Miley; she was so busy filming *Hannah Montana* and touring that it was almost impossible to fit it in but somehow she managed it. She arrived on set as a single girl, as she had just ended her relationship with Justin Gaston, but she left deeply in love with Liam Hemsworth.

Miley never expected to fall for an actor and had even said to journalists in the past that she would never date one. Her opinion changed when she met Liam on the set of *The Last Song*, which was filmed on the isolated Tybee Island in Savannah, Georgia. To begin with they did keep their relationship a secret from the rest of the cast and the crew because they wanted to be professional. That said, many of their co-workers guessed something was going on because they had such great chemistry. Miley and Liam would hang out once the cameras stopped rolling and their friendship soon grew into something more.

Liam was born in Melbourne, Australia and is three years older than Miley. He started his acting career on TV shows, playing Josh Taylor in *Neighbours* and Marcus in *The Elephant Princess*. He has two brothers, Luke and Chris, who are both actors. Luke is best known for playing Nathan Tyson in *Neighbours* and Chris is best known for playing Thor in the Marvel films.

DID YOU KNOW?

Liam actually auditioned to play Thor but lost out to his older brother Chris.

Miley and Liam kissed for the first time on their initial day of filming. They hardly knew each other to talk to, let alone kiss. Liam explained to Ryan Seacrest, 'We turned up on set the very first day and originally it was just a scene where we were running through the water and splashing and having fun. And halfway through the scene, the director, Julie Anne, she yelled "Kiss!" And we got thrown into a kiss on the boat. It was good, 'cause, you know, [you] get the first one out of the way, and it was fine.'

Liam is a huge 6ft 4in so he is the tallest guy that Miley has dated. He was also the first that wasn't American. Miley gushed to *Popstar!* magazine when they first started dating, 'Liam is so much fun to work with! The crazy thing is he's such a huge star in Australia, and so to help introduce him to our side of the world was really cool. I know how that feels because I travel all over the world on tour and I'm more well known here than I am in some of the places I've visited. So I totally know where he's coming from!'

Liam told the same magazine, 'Miley is great! We had a lot of fun, she's always bright and happy and it's a pleasure to work with her. We got along really well and became good friends during the shoot.'

DID YOU KNOW?

Miley was intimidated by Liam's height when she first met him. She thought she'd have to get boxes to stand on all the time. She also knew that he was a big star in Australia so she was a bit nervous about acting alongside him in the beginning but, once they started, she realised that he was just a nice, down-to-earth guy.

The director, producers and cast all thought Miley did an amazing job but she herself wasn't 100 per cent happy and thought she still needed acting lessons. Before filming was completed she told reporters that she'd book an acting coach once she had seen the film. She wanted to hone her craft and become a great adult actress; she didn't just want to be good, she wanted to be great.

Miley had decided to record 'When I Look At You' for her album but it ended up being the film's biggest and most memorable song. She told *MyParkMag* what happened: 'When we realised it describes this entire movie, we had a composer come in and make a piano piece for me to be able to play. It's in the movie when Ronnie reveals to Will that she plays the piano. It was perfect for that scene because it's a love song, but it's also about God, about family, about love – it's kind of what this movie is all about.'

Miley's mom Tish was the executive producer on the film so she had a big role to play on set. Miley and her family have their own production company called Cyrus' Hope Town Entertainment, which has a production deal with Disney. Miley isn't the first star to have her own production company. Taylor Lautner has one with his dad, and other big stars like Jennifer Aniston and Tom Cruise have their own too. It helps them keep control over the films they make.

Miley loved the time she spent in Tybee filming *The Last Song*. She told *Harper's Bazaar*, 'I went out every night with my friends. I did karaoke. I danced. All this stuff would've been such a big deal in Los Angeles: Who's she with? Why is she dancing? I felt alive and real. It's so much easier to know who you are when there aren't a thousand people telling you who they think you are. I felt like I was really figuring myself out. Usually I have someone whispering in my ear, but I was on my own.'

DID YOU KNOW?

When they were filming *The Last Song*, Miley and Chris ate out at a restaurant called Stingrays every night and they loved the seafood there. Miley ordered the crabs' legs because she liked snapping them, letting all her aggression out in the process. She and Liam liked the people too and Miley even performed there on a couple of nights. Liam didn't though because he's not a singer by any stretch of the imagination.

Miley was really sad on the final day of filming *The Last Song*. She didn't want to have to say goodbye to Liam so she was over the moon when he said he would go to Nashville for a while so they could hang out.

Billy Ray and Tish were happy that Miley had met Liam and thought he was really nice. Miley said, 'My dad's just happy that I have something going on in my life with someone normal. No psychos, so that's good.'

In *The Last Song* Ronnie's mom was played by John Travolta's wife Kelly Preston. Kelly and John have been good friends of the Cyrus family for a long time and Miley was the one who encouraged her to take the role. She had been going through a terrible time because her young son Jett had died only a few months before but after speaking to Miley, she felt that the time might be right to act again. Kelly told *People* magazine she did it 'because Miley asked me herself to play her mom. I was really moved. It was the perfect movie to sort of get my feet wet.'

Kelly's daughter Ella was thrilled because she's a big Miley fan and got to hang around the set. Even though both families had been friends for a while, it was during the filming of *The Last Song* that they got super-close.

Because Ronnie is a talented pianist it was thought that Miley would need lots of piano lessons so that she could play the piano in the movie. She had played occasionally in the past when she was a young girl because her pappy had a piano in his log cabin but she had never had lessons or read music while playing; she just made up her own tunes. However, Miley impressed everyone with how quickly she mastered the instrument after only a couple of lessons.

'Maybe it was easier because I already play guitar. I learned not just how to play a song but how to play it like a classically trained musician, the way to sit, the way you look when you're at the piano, the posture, the fingering,' she explained. 'It's a lot more disciplined than just casual playing. The learning experiences are a part of my job I really love. So many people dream of learning something like this and I'm getting this experience along with making a movie.'

DID YOU KNOW?

Miley had to swim with sharks for one scene in the film, which she was understandably really nervous about. The workers at Georgia Aquarium had told her that they hadn't fed the sharks for a few days to make sure that they would swim close to her, which would panic anybody. She also had to master the skill of scuba diving since she had never done that before.

Miley was extremely excited about the release of *The Last Song* because she wanted to show people that she could act. Her fans thought her portrayal of Ronnie was brilliant but film critics were less than complimentary, slating her acting skills. They seemed to treat her more harshly than they might treat other actresses of her young age. Thankfully, Miley has her great family, friends and fans to help her through these tough times.

She confessed to BBC News,

I'm a very positive person, I'm super-spiritual and I'm just very connected. If you have a positive mind, you'll live a positive life. I surround myself with positivity. I don't really look at the reviews because I'm very proud of the film. I don't think anyone can really look at the movie and say this film doesn't have a message or this film is useless and was a waste of an hour and a half.

It's like my music, you don't have to listen to it, you don't have to watch it. Don't ever let anyone ever tell you that something you did isn't good if you're proud of it.

DID YOU KNOW?

Miley couldn't go to the UK premiere of *The Last Song* in April 2010 because there were no flights in or out of the UK at the time, due to volcanic ash clouds that had made their way to the UK from Iceland.

While promoting the film, poor Liam had to put up with interviewers who had trouble understanding his Australian accent and mistakenly thought that he was saying his name was Leon. Rather than getting upset about it, he and Miley decided to make a joke of it and she gave him the nickname Kevin.

DID YOU KNOW?

The *Transformers* actor Josh Duhamel might be married to Black Eyed Peas singer Fergie but that didn't stop Miley winding him up on a flight from Los Angeles to London. She found out that she could send text messages to other passengers on the flight via their seats, so sent Josh a few cheeky messages. She called up

---

Ryan Seacrest's radio show to tell him all about it: 'I was, like, "Hey, stud!" He didn't know which seat I was in, so I could tell him all these funny things [without being discovered]. He didn't text me back [because] it was rude.'

CHAPTER EIGHT

WONDER WORLD

Miley released 'Party in the USA' on 11 August 2009 and it became a huge hit. It reached number 2 in the USA, number 3 in New Zealand and Canada, number 4 in Japan, number 5 in Ireland, number 6 in France, Australia and Hungary, and number 11 in the UK.

Initially, she had been unsure about the song. Originally it had been written for Jessie J but she had decided against recording it because she didn't think it was 'edgy' enough. But Miley needed more tracks for her album *The Time of Our Lives* so agreed to include it after producer Dr. Luke gave it a working over.

Miley must have been blown away by how popular the song became the second it was released. It was on the radio constantly and fans loved the *Grease*-inspired video. It was a surprise hit for Miley because she'd initially released it to promote her clothing line for Walmart.

DID YOU KNOW?

Miley was excited about having her own range of clothes stocked in Walmart until she attended a meeting and saw the clothes the store had decided to include in her range. Her excitement soon turned to disappointment. She had wanted her range to include jeggings and skinny jeans but it wasn't to be in the end.

Even though 'Party in the USA' did brilliantly, it isn't perhaps as special to Miley as some others, as she played no part in the writing process. 'Party in the USA' was written by Lukasz Gottwald, Claude Kelly and Jessica Cornish. She might sing about Jay-Z on the track but, when she first picked the song, Miley had apparently never heard a Jay-Z track.

DID YOU KNOW?

The video for 'Party in the USA' won the MuchMusic Video Award for Best International Artist Video.

Miley first performed 'Party in the USA' live at the 2009 Teen Choice Awards on 10 August 2009. She hadn't expected her high-energy performance to be controversial but, when she danced around a pole on top of an ice-cream cart, she was criticised for pole dancing in front of impressionable teens. Critics said her performance was highly suggestive but, in fact, it was remarkably tame. Miley mostly used the pole as a support as her dancers wheeled her around the stage.

Her outfit consisted of a vest, black hot pants and biker boots. There was a small glimpse of the side strap of Miley's bra but the outfit was age appropriate and was no different to what many of the girls in the audience were wearing. This didn't stop the critics complaining, though.

Before Miley took to the stage she told Larry Carroll from MTV: '[My] performance tonight is funny, but I wanted it to be about [something more]. "Party in the USA" is an all-American song, and so I come out tonight and I'm literally in a trailer park. It's a blinged-out trailer park.'

For Miley, it was important that her performance reflected her roots. She explained, 'I'm like, "This is to represent where I am from." I'm so proud of it... All the girls trying to be Hollywood and stuff with their big glasses, me shooing them away.'

The day after her performance Newsday.com reported that a Disney Channel representative had said, 'Disney Channel won't be commenting on that performance, although parents can rest assured that all content presented on the Disney Channel is age appropriate for our audience – kids 6–14 – and consistent with what our brand values are.'

They also spoke to child psychologist Wendi Fischer, who thought that Miley was showing her fans that it is acceptable to pole dance. She commented, 'She's sending this message that this is "OK" to do, and I don't think it is OK to do... Miley's only sixteen. Why is she rushing it?'

The majority of Smilers thought that the media's reaction was extreme and didn't feel that Miley was being too sexual. They wanted to praise her for everything she achieved that night: picking up six awards was a tremendous achievement. Miley won two awards for *Hannah Montana: The Movie*, two awards for *Hannah Montana* and two awards for her singles 'The Climb' and 'Before the Storm'. Her dad also won an award for his role as Miley's dad in *Hannah Montana* and Emily Osment won an award for playing best sidekick.

Only a few weeks after the Teen Choice Awards Miley embarked on her second tour, the Wonder World Tour. It kicked off on 14 September 2009 and finished three months later on 29 December. There were 56 dates: 45 in North America and 11 covering England and Ireland.

DID YOU KNOW?

Miley rode a luggage cart instead of an ice-cream cart during her tour performances of 'Party in the USA'.

For this tour Miley performed solely as herself and was supported by her brother Trace and his band Metro Station. Miley's managers had been nervous about allowing Trace to perform because of his tattoos. Trace explained to OrangeCounty.com in February 2012, 'People don't expect me to make pop music. Even on the tour with Miley, her managers and people on her label didn't even want us [there]. Not because of our music but because of the way I looked. That bothers me more than anything.

'Some of the most successful artists are the weirdest ones – look at Lady Gaga. I've done shows with her and she's amazing. When people first meet me, they think I'm going to be a mean guy or something. I guess I just need to prove that you can't judge a book by its cover.'

Miley was touring around the time of her birthday but she had the night off and her parents surprised her with an eighties-themed party in New York. Miley's cake was huge: there were four tiers and a mini-rock band made of icing performing on it. The cast of the musical *Rock of Ages* dropped by and performed for her and her guests. There might have been fewer people there than at her sixteenth birthday party the year before but she still had an amazing time.

DID YOU KNOW?

While in the UK, Miley was given the special job of opening the 2009 Royal Variety Show with a performance of 'Party in the USA'. She was really excited before the big night and told people she wanted to teach HM the Queen the 'Hoedown Throwdown'!

Miley's Wonder World show was divided into seven segments, with each segment having a different theme. She only had three weeks to rehearse before hitting the road because she'd been busy filming *The Last Song*, so she was under a lot of pressure. The show was directed by Jamal Sims and he also choreographed a lot of Miley's dance routines. He was assisted by fourteen other choreographers/ directors who made up Miley's creative team, including Octavius Terry and Dondraico Johnson.

DID YOU KNOW?

Miley likes to raise as much money as she can for charity so, for every concert ticket sold, she donated $1 to the cancer charity City of Hope National Medical Center.

Wonder World Tour Set List:

1. Breakout
2. Start All Over
3. 7 Things
4. Kicking and Screaming
5. Bottom of the Ocean
6. Fly on the Wall
7. Thriller (Dance interlude)
8. Let's Get Crazy
9. Hoedown Throwdown
10. Boom Boom Pow (Dance interlude)
11. These Four Walls
12. When I Look at You
13. Obsessed
14. Spotlight
15. G.N.O (Girl's Night Out)
16. I Love Rock 'n' Roll
17. Party in the USA
18. Hovering
19. Simple Song
20. See You Again
21. The Climb

When Miley is going through tough times she likes to write songs. It allows her to express herself, let off steam and help focus her mind, so singing and songwriting provide her with an outlet for her emotions. Not all of Miley's songs have been released; some are just personal ones that she can play on her own if she wants.

DID YOU KNOW?

Miley was writing a book called *The Diary of Priscilla's Coffeehouse* about some people she met in a coffee shop. She was never planning to publish it, she just wanted to write it for herself. She has never revealed in interviews whether she ever finished it.

When Miley started out writing pop songs she would begin by making beats and then add lyrics to them. Her ballads usually came together from notes she had made about how she was feeling at a particular time. She didn't set out to turn how she was feeling into songs but sometimes it just happened that way: she'd be writing and suddenly think, 'That would make a good song and help people going through a similar situation.'

Miley released '7 Things' on 17 June 2008. It was the first song she released from the album and was a big hit worldwide – it appeared in the top 10 in the US, Japan, Australia and Norway. When her fans listened to the song, many instantly thought it was about Nick Jonas because he and Miley had recently broken up after their two-year relationship.

Popstar! magazine asked her about the rumours. Miley

said, '[With] "7 Things" I think a lot of people do, you know, think it's about Nick Jonas, and if they think it is, that's fine, or whoever they think it's about. But mostly that song is about who, um, they want it to be... Like mostly, it's if a girl hates her current, or ex-boyfriend – for me it's an ex-boyfriend – so I think, you know, like, Nick is someone that was really important in my life, but I don't hate him. It's a good song and it's fun.'

Miley might have written the song because of Nick but he certainly didn't think it was aimed at him when he heard it because of some of the lyrics. He doesn't think he was insecure at all and he doesn't think his friends are uncool!

DID YOU KNOW?

In 2008 Miley earned her first MTV VMA nomination for Best New Artist for her single '7 Things'. She arrived at the ceremony with Taylor Swift and Katy Perry, who were also up for the award, but all three ladies lost out to the band Tokio Hotel.

Miley has always been crazy about Christmas so it was really hard for her to be away for Christmas 2009 due to her touring schedule. She loves spending time with her family, getting presents, eating good food and, with Miley and her family being devout Christians, it is, of course, an important celebration of the birth of Jesus. It is a fun time when she can just be herself and chill out at home with her family.

She told Pete Wentz that Christmas in the Cyrus family is 'nuts because we've got Trace, who is always on tour who comes in and it's kind of like something new, we're not used to having a rock star in our house... I'm not as demanding as he is and I take nowhere near as long to get ready, but that's really fun. And we like just being together because it's all about music at Christmas time. Dad sings them [carols].'

Christmas 2009 was also all about music, albeit in a very different setting because she was busy performing in the UK in December and January. At first she was nervous not to be celebrating Christmas at home in the US and worried that the food might be different. She was, however, relieved to find that people in the UK eat turkey too.

DID YOU KNOW?

Miley was able to visit a lot of countries as she promoted Hannah Montana around the world. She had a world map at home that she added stickers to every time she visited a different country. Her big ambition was to visit as many countries as possible, even if it was just the once.

Miley stayed at the Soho Hotel for the majority of her time in London but she was originally going to be staying in an apartment her team had rented for her as her European base. However, she found the apartment far too scary, as she explained to *Elle* magazine: 'It was seriously so terrifying. One night, my little sister – it sounds crazy to tell you – but she was standing in the shower and all of a sudden, I hear her scream. I run in there and the water had somehow flipped to hot but it was still... It wasn't like the water had just changed, the knob had turned but she hadn't turned it and it was burning her. She was really red.'

This incident on its own probably wouldn't have caused Miley to relocate but when she thought she saw a little boy watching her take a shower, she knew she couldn't stay in the apartment one minute longer. She revealed, 'I was sitting there the next night and maybe I'm crazy, but I could have sworn I could see this little boy sitting there on the sink, kicking his feet.'

The apartment was in an historic building and after investigating the history of the place, Miley came to the conclusion that the boy must have been the son of the man who had owned it. She vowed never to stay there again!

As she jetted from one country to the next promoting Hannah Montana, she clocked up thousands of air miles. She tried to catch up on sleep or read a book during the flights. It was actually nice for her to have some time to chill but being in a different country every day was sometimes confusing as she would constantly wake up in new and unfamiliar places.

CHAPTER NINE
CAN'T BE TAMED

Miley got her second tattoo in early 2010 after accompanying her dad to a tattoo parlour. While Billy Ray was getting a tattoo, she decided to have the word 'LOVE' tattooed inside her right ear. The decision to have the tattoo in her ear was for a very important reason, as she explained to *Access Hollywood*: 'I have "Love" right here to block out all the crap that everyone throws into your ears... I don't really care about it. [You're] only supposed to hear the things coming from the people that genuinely love you.'

In a separate interview with *E! News* she said, 'There's so much negativity in the world and what you only need to hear is all the love. People try to say to me, "I just heard someone say this or that about you," and I just ignore it because it's irrelevant. Love is what makes the world go around and that's all we need to focus on.'

Miley liked living with her family but since her early teens she always wanted her independence and looked forward to moving out and getting her own place. Initially, Tish had made her promise to live at home until she was twenty but there was no way Miley could wait that long.

She bought her first home in the spring of 2010 when she was seventeen and the press speculated that it had cost a cool $3.4 million. The house in Toluca Lake, Los Angeles was only two blocks away from her parents' home so Tish didn't have to worry too much about Miley. It had four bedrooms, five bathrooms, a swimming pool and a tennis court; also its very own recording studio and a separate guest building with two more bedrooms.

Liam Hemsworth joked to *People* magazine that he was going to help her decorate, saying, 'I could come in and gather some pictures of myself to put on her wall and see what she says. I'll sign it for her as well, and it will say, "Dear Miley, best wishes with the new house!"'

Joking aside, Miley did get some help when it came to decorating the house. Before she moved in she told *People* magazine, 'My house is going to be gorgeous because my mom is an interior designer. It's like if your mom's a clothes designer you're always going to look great. My mom's an interior designer so my house is going to be perfect all the time.' Miley wanted the house to feel informal and welcoming so opted for cool low-seat couches and huge cushions on the floor, so she could just chill out when people called by to see her. She didn't want a lot of fussy items and things that could break; she wanted her friends to see her home as a place they could visit any time they wanted.

Miley is a huge animal fan and especially loves dogs. When she first moved to LA, she and her sister Brandi actually tried to set up their own dog-walking service but it didn't work out because no one would hire them. They put up signs everywhere but they didn't get a single phone call. Miley used to joke that, if she stopped acting and singing, she would become a professional dog walker.

When Miley was growing up, her family had a lot of dogs. They had a German Shepherd called Texas T (or Tex), who was Billy Ray's favourite and travelled with him everywhere. Also a Shih Tzu called Loco, who was Noah's favourite and lived with them in LA. They had another German Shepherd called Rosie, who lived in Nashville, a Labrador-and-Beagle cross called Fluke, who split his time between LA and Nashville, and a black Shih Tzu called Juicy. When Miley was thirteen, she visited the Houston Rodeo Show and bought a Yorkshire Terrier, whom they named Rodeo (or Roadie). The year after that she acquired another Yorkshire Terrier called Shooter. When she turned sixteen, she was given a Maltese-Poodle cross puppy, who she called Sofie after her granddad's dog. Not long afterwards, she got Mate, a white German Shepherd – naming him Mate because that was one of Liam's nick-names (he says 'mate' a lot!).

When she was in *Hannah Montana*, Miley had a white rabbit called Jack, who lived with her in LA, seven horses that lived in Nashville (Memphis being her favourite), three cats, which also lived in Nashville, twelve birds, a donkey, a goat called Billy and a gecko.

When Miley moved out and got her own place, she didn't take her dogs with her because they were settled, living with Tish and Billy Ray. She decided to adopt dogs instead and she encourages everyone who is thinking of getting a dog to adopt a dog from a shelter rather than to buy from a breeder.

For Miley, a dog's personality is more important than the way it looks: she likes dogs who are super-affectionate and enjoy going on long walks. That said, several of her dogs are picture perfect. When she adopted Floyd in July 2011, she tweeted her followers a photo of herself cuddling him, with the message, 'I'm so in love with him it is ridiculous.'

DID YOU KNOW?

When the paparazzi snap Miley around Los Angeles, she is normally nipping out to get some dog food or going for a walk in the park – she would much rather snuggle on the couch with her fur babies than go clubbing.

In February 2012 Miley tweeted songwriter and producer Antonina Armato, who co-wrote/produced '7 Things', 'See You Again' and 'Fly on the Wall', to say, 'Why would I need human friends? Dude, Lila will ALWAYS love me and that's more than we can say about most humans.'

Miley was inspired to move out of her parents' home and start rescuing dogs by Demi Moore when they worked on *LOL* together in 2010/11. Demi had offered Miley some advice, telling her to find herself a sanctuary as she herself had done before she had her children, Rumer, Scout LaRue and Tallulah Belle. Miley explained to *Viva Press*,

I was so inspired by working with her. One thing that she did that I really loved was when she – a few years ago when she first started having a baby – she went away and lived on a farm and spent time away because she just wanted to raise her family and raise them somewhere other than LA which is later down the line that's something that is really important to me. I don't necessarily want to ever have a family here and grow up here. It's scary out there. It's a war zone. She kind of told me that's what she did.

So when I got home, I got a little puppy dog and I bought a house and I moved out and I just wanted to stay there in my own sanctuary and make it a place that I don't have to leave besides to go to the grocery store and that's about it. I now have four dogs. I love being home with my pets. I don't really want to leave. She really taught me to have that place, have that one place that's yours. That no one can come on there. That's your space. It's beautiful being able to have a place.

DID YOU KNOW?

Miley adopted her black-and-tan mongrel Happy after finding him abandoned outside a Walmart. She tweeted, 'I don't understand how people can be so cruel. That's why we named him Happy.'

Miley was given the great honour of presenting at the Oscars on 7 March 2010. She presented the Best Original Song Oscar with *Mamma Mia!* star Amanda Seyfried. Both looked stunning in their long gowns, although Miley seemed a bit nervous as she presented the award. But who can blame her? There were 41 million people watching her on TV!

Miley felt privileged to record a duet with Bret Michaels from the band Poison. Her mum is a huge Poison fan and she took Miley to see the band in concert when she was younger. Miley recorded 'Nothin' to Lose' with Bret for his album *Custom Built*, and it was released as a single on 2 March 2010. When some critics heard that they had recorded 'Nothin' to Lose' together, they decided to attack Miley and Bret, claiming the lyrics were unsuitable as Miley was a young girl and Bret thirty years her senior.

The two singers couldn't believe how much the critics blew it out of proportion. Bret had written the song years before and hadn't intended for it be sung as a duet, and Miley's mum Tish had been in the studio with them during the recording. There was no scandal!

Miley's third album of her own was called *Can't Be Tamed* and was released on 18 June 2010. One of its tracks is a cover version of Poison's 'Every Rose Has Its Thorn'. *Can't Be Tamed* was first released in Germany, Australia and Poland before being released in the UK and USA three days later, on 21 June. Miley was involved in the writing of all the tracks but was also helped by some great songwriters.

The album reached number 2 in Austria, Canada and New Zealand, number 3 in the USA, number 4 in Australia and Germany, and number 5 in Ireland.

Track Listing:
1. Liberty Walk
2. Who Owns My Heart
3. Can't Be Tamed
4. Every Rose Has Its Thorn
5. Two More Lonely People
6. Forgiveness and Love
7. Permanent December
8. Stay
9. Scars
10. Take Me Along
11. Robot
12. My Heart Beats for Love

Miley gushed on American talk show *Live With Regis and Kelly*, 'I work with really good people, you know, that I'm able to collaborate with and so it's someone to look at and look up to and they have good opinions but they also, you know, are totally OK when I say, "No, I know that this is the way I want it to sound." Because, at the end of the day, it's got my name on it.'

Miley wrote the title track 'Can't Be Tamed' with two of her closest friends and she liked the way the song reflected how she felt after leaving *Hannah Montana* – she couldn't be tamed anymore. She wasn't going to let people try to put her in a box and define her. She wasn't a Disney kid anymore; she was an independent woman with her own ideas and her own aspirations. The message behind the song is one of Miley following her heart to produce the kind of music she wants to, rather than what other people think she should. Through the lyrics and the video, she wanted to show her fans that they should be bold and unafraid of being creative and expressing themselves. She wanted to help them deal with the pressure they might sometimes feel in trying to live up to their parents' expectations.

The video for 'Can't Be Tamed' was much sexier than Miley's previous videos. With her friend and choreographer Jamal Sims, she came up with the concept of playing a rare creature stuck in captivity. They explained their ideas to director Robert Hales, who had previously worked with Justin Timberlake, Kings of Leon, Britney Spears, Jonas Brothers and many more top performers. He thought their concept was great and added some of his own personal touches to make the video one of the most memorable of 2010.

In the video Miley and her dancers wear some gorgeous costumes. The silver corset Miley herself wears cost an incredible $25,000 and was made out of metal and feathers. She had to give it back as soon as filming finished, which was a real shame because she would have loved to keep it.

DID YOU KNOW?

Shooting the video for 'Can't Be Tamed' was a bit daunting for Miley because her boyfriend at the time, Liam Hemsworth, brought his mum and dad along to watch. Miley's only previous meetings with Liam's parents had been while relaxing in Australia, so it must have been a strange experience for them all.

A slightly nervous Miley promoting Hannah Montana.

Left: Miley can't stop smiling after getting her dream job in 2006.

Right: Attending a film premiere with her dad Billy Ray.

Above left: When Miley goes to big events she loves having her mum and dad by her side.

Above right: Miley will always have an unbreakable bond with her mum, Tish, and her little sister, Noah.

Below: Miley's family mean the world to her; they've always encouraged her to dream big.

Above left: Miley waves to the crowd dressed as Hannah Montana.

Above right: Miley celebrated her Sweet Sixteen in style at Disney World.

Below left: Performing for the Queen of England is something Miley will never forget.

Below right: Miley feels so alive when she's singing for her Smilers.

Miley loves getting dressed up for award shows and she always looks incredibly glamorous.

Left: Promoting *The Last Song* around the world with Liam was a very special time for Miley.

Right: Miley and Liam were a happy couple, smiling for the cameras at the Vanity Fair Oscar Party.

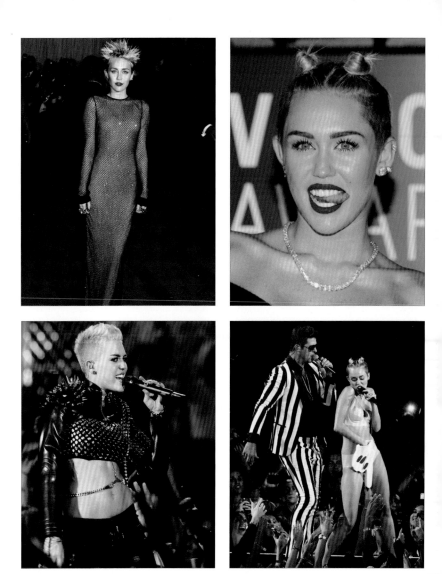

Above left: The world was shocked when Miley arrived in a nearly nude punk dress at the Met Gala in 2013.

Above right: Her trademark tongue is almost as famous as Miley now, and is putting in an appearance on the red carpet here.

Below left: Now she's grown up and independent, when Miley takes to the stage she looks a bit different from her Hannah Montana years.

Below right: Twerking with Robin Thicke at the MTV VMAs was very controversial, but Miley instantly became the biggest star on the planet.

Welcome to
Miley's world!
Bangerz style!

Miley said, when she released the song, that she never wants to disrespect *Hannah Montana* because it has made her who she is today but that, in many ways, doing the show had made her feel like a bird in a cage with clipped wings. She couldn't do all the things she wanted to do because she had to protect the Disney brand.

This train of thought is echoed on Miley's album track 'Robot'. It talks about having your life dictated by others – being told how to behave, how to look, what you can and can't do – and about leaving that life behind in order to make your own decisions. Miley wants people to show their independence and not care what others think. She said at the time that she thought a lot of songs in the charts were about 'nothing' – just going out and finding guys. Miley wanted to show that there's more to life than that. She isn't against that type of song but just wanted to write songs that go deeper.

On 21 June 2010 Miley performed an MTV live-stream concert at the House of Blues in Los Angeles. It was a chance to show the audience how much she had changed since the release of her first Hannah Montana album, back in 2006. She pretended to kiss one of her female dancers and, when introducing her song 'Heart Beats for Love', she explained that she wrote it mostly for her gay fans, adding she hates that 'we have people on this earth who hate someone for loving another'. As she sang Miley made the peace sign, which was soon copied by the Smilers in the audience, who were blown away by her performances of 'Can't Be Tamed', 'Who Owns My Heart', 'Liberty Walk', 'Every Rose Has Its Thorn', 'Robot' and 'Heart Beats for Love'.

She explained to Sway Calloway from MTV, 'I'm a

completely different person. I'm so much more confident. I've always been a confident person. I was going through a lot then... I was younger. I didn't really know myself and there are so many people telling you who you should and shouldn't be and that's what "Tamed" is about. It's about being who you are to the full and now I know who that is.'

DID YOU KNOW?

When Miley reached puberty and developed breasts, she had to put up with people bandaging her chest so that she would still have a younger-looking figure for *Hannah Montana*. The people in charge didn't want Hannah Montana to grow up as quickly as Miley.

Liam and Miley split for the first time in August 2010, shortly after their one-year anniversary.

Miley admitted to *Marie Claire* in 2012, 'Liam and I have a really good relationship. It took breaking up once or twice because I was young and immature and wanted to do things I hadn't yet gotten to do. He was older, so it was like he'd already been through school. At some point you realize these people you're hanging out with are your "party friends"; they're not going to give a s**t about you in ten years. Then you remember who you really want around you.'

Miley's next film role was in *LOL*. Although she started filming in the summer of 2010 the film wasn't released until 1 June 2012 in the UK. She played the lead character, Lola (or Lol, for short), who is struggling with the ups and downs of high school after her boyfriend meets someone else. Her mother, Anne (played by Demi Moore), is newly single and does her best to try and make sure Lol is OK. The film is a remake of a 2008 French film, with the same director as the original, Lisa Azuelos.

LOL was mainly filmed in Chicago, where the story is set, but some scenes were shot in Detroit and they wrapped in Paris. Lisa Azuelos also cast the film and chose actors and actresses who touched her heart. She explained to AnythingDiz, 'It's very unfair, because a person enters the room and I know if he's going to do the movie or not. In one second, it's intuitive. So I chose them by heart... They enter the room, I love them, and I ask them to do the movie. And when they say, "Yes," it's great.' She said Miley was:

Very professional and a great example on set. She was known to always be the first one there and ready to go... Miley was on set when they told her she didn't have to be [this was a 15-hour day]. She wasn't being filmed for most of the day, the other actors were somewhere else because they weren't being filmed, but she mingled with the extras, interacted with the cast who was being filmed and the crew, studied her script, etc. She knew her lines, she was on top of her game, and she took her craft very seriously.

I just love Miley so much. First of all, she's so gifted... Naturally, if she's where she is today it's not because she's been lucky. It's because she's pure energy: heart and joy. I think that people love her for good reason. She brings love to people. And people really love her in return. I'm not sure I had it that much in the French movie, but here I have chemistry between Demi and

Miley that is absolutely out of control. And I didn't create that. The two of them act like they've been in the same room since Miley was born. Although Miley and Demi don't really look alike physically, they look alike in the same room. They're like mother and daughter. I've been so lucky that both of them did the movie.

Miley can see a lot of similarities between herself and her character Lola. One of them is that they both have strong females in their lives. She revealed, 'I've always had a really good relationship with my mom. But it's good when you can also have another woman in your life that you can go to and talk to, as well – one that is like a mother figure, but also just a friend with no expectations. And you can just say whatever like... On random days I'll get a text from Demi when I may be down. And I'll get a text like, "Your second mom loves you." And that'll just turn your day around.'

Miley loves filming in the summer months because she can spend the rest of the year touring and promoting her music. When shooting, she likes to be in the same place for a few months so as to get to know the cast and the crew and form a new 'film family'. Miley becomes so attached to her surrogate families that she finds it difficult when they all have to go their separate ways at the end of filming.

Before they started shooting *LOL* Miley was counting down the days because she was so excited. It was like nothing she'd ever done before and she was looking forward to doing an independent film without having a studio attached. Everyone could just concentrate on making a great film without the added pressures that having a big studio involved brings.

Miley had to film a sex scene for the film with actor Douglas Booth, who plays Kyle. She admitted that she was nervous at first but that her nerves soon passed. She had forgotten to shave her legs that day, so quickly shaved them before filming started. When she was asked how she prepared for it in an interview for the *Sun*, Miley replied, 'Breath mints, stomach crunches, spray tan. Plus workouts to make my boobs look bigger, perk them up.'

Douglas found it tough doing the scene with Miley because it took place on their first day of filming. He really liked Miley but thinks they are very different people. He explained to the *Telegraph*, 'Miley is great, she's in a completely different stratosphere from me, and moves in completely different circles.'

Miley loved teasing Douglas during filming and in down time. She told Viva Press,

Yeah. He's gorgeous. He's like one of the coolest dudes ever. He's really funny. We always called him princess because he had like this – it's like anywhere like anyone with an accent but he has like a very posh English accent. It seems like old Shakespeare or something. We went out on these really crappy jet skis one day and he's like, 'This is no St Barts.' I'm like whatever. I'm like, 'You princess. You've been living in London way too long.' He like comes in and we're going on a boat, he's got like his shirt tucked in perfectly and everything. How do you look perfect? We're all like sweaty and gross and like laying out and you like coming here and looking like a perfect model, which you are. We always called him princess. It was hilarious.

The film raises some questions about teenagers and sex and, during an interview with Amanda de Cadenet, Miley wasn't afraid to discuss the matter. She said, 'The girls that really base how much they're worth on the sexual favours they can do for somebody, that makes me really sad. Because sex is actually really beautiful. It's the only way we create, and it's the only way the world keeps going.'

She thinks the overarching message of the film is 'Always remember that you're growing up and that growing up means you'll make some mistakes. Don't blame yourself. Don't even think of it as a mistake. Think of it as an experience. It's like having a little scar. It's good. It gives you character. Then when you're older and you have kids or whatever, remember to understand and to remember what you felt then.'

DID YOU KNOW?

When promoting the film, Miley chatted to Viva Press about losing her virginity. She said, 'I think it does change you as a person a little bit because in a way you start thinking maybe that's like what guys want from you a little bit. You start feeling things differently as a woman, when you're looked at differently and whatever. I think it is a big part of growing up because it opens a whole new connection and heartbreak.'

Miley and Demi Moore had great fun shooting *LOL* but Demi always knew they would because Miley is so grounded and easy to get along with. She also liked having the opportunity to meet the whole Cyrus family. Demi told MTV, 'Miley is a true professional and she truly has a wonderful family... it really shows.'

Miley got her third tattoo during the filming of *LOL*, at a tattoo parlour on 8 Mile, Detroit – and it was the first she'd had done without her mum's permission. She kept it a secret from Tish for two months by covering it with a plaster.

The tattoo is the outline of a small heart on the little finger on her right hand. It is now a Cyrus family tradition to get a heart tattoo on your hand – Billy Ray, Tish, Trace and Brandi all have one. Noah and Braison will no doubt get heart tattoos when they are old enough.

The tradition started when Miley drew a heart on Billy Ray's hand during a church service, back in 2008. Billy Ray had decided that particular Sunday was 'Miley's day' so, when she suggested they visit a tattoo parlour, he agreed and decided to have her drawing turned into a permanent reminder. Everyone's tattoo is slightly different: his is positioned between his thumb and index finger and is filled in, Brandi's is in the same position but larger, Trace's is on his thumb and Tish's is on her little finger and is pink.

The delay in the release of *LOL* frustrated the director, producers, Miley and everyone involved in the production. The wait was caused by a number of factors. Although the film was shown in selected cinemas, when the controversy surrounding Miley's eighteenth birthday broke, a larger release was cancelled. The producers decided an urgent edit was needed as in one scene Miley's character smokes with her friends. They managed to edit the scene in such a way that it doesn't appear as if Miley is smoking.

Another factor that led to the delay was that the company who had made the film didn't have the resources to promote it as much as they might have. They were working on the much bigger blockbuster movie *The Hunger Games* and needed to focus on that first. At the premiere of *The Hunger Games* Miley chatted about *LOL* to Ben Lyons from *Extra*. She said, 'It's a small indie film that I wanted to make because I loved the script and I love the director, Lisa Azuelos. That's really why I took this on. I'm really excited for people to see it.'

It was such a shame that *LOL* didn't receive the right publicity because it had so much potential. The French version had been a huge hit and the US version showcased how well Miley could act. It was released in only 105 cinemas in the US, on the same weekend that blockbuster *The Avengers* was released. *LOL* never stood a chance against the competition and only took $46,500 over the whole weekend. It was a big flop and pretty much went straight to DVD.

Despite it failing to cause even a ripple in the film world, Miley was still glad she did the movie and tweeted Smilers who did go to see it in the cinema to thank them. She wrote, 'Thank u so much for everyone who went to see LOL.

'It is a film I loved making and I am proud of... That's really all that matters to me.'

The director Lisa Azuelos was understandably

disappointed and told *The Los Angeles Times*, 'I really thought this movie could be universal... usually teen movies are tender or scary or have vampires in them, but they're never realistic. This story isn't too dirty and not too stupid.'

As well as playing the lead roles in *The Last Song* and *LOL*, Miley also filmed a cameo for *Sex and the City 2*. In the film Miley plays herself on a red carpet, wearing the exact same dress as Samantha (played by Kim Cattrall). They both look shocked and embarrassed but, instead of trying to hide, they pose for photos together and make the best of a bad situation.

Miley might not have had a big part but she was excited to be involved and to have the opportunity to meet Sarah Jessica Parker, Kim Cattrall, Kristin Davis and Cynthia Nixon.

They were equally excited to meet Miley. Sarah Jessica Parker told MTV, 'Did you know that she's tall? She's like a Viking. I had no idea! She's a beautiful young lady and very self-possessed. I literally was not in the scene with her. I was in the scene, but we were not [on screen] together. But she was lovely and on time and professional, very sweet. She worked two hours and she was in and out.'

Miley told Ryan Seacrest on his 102.7 KIIS FM radio show, 'It was literally like the best job I've ever done and it was like a total dream come true. It was so cool... working with Kim [Cattrall] was really cool and Sarah Jessica Parker was like the nicest person in the world.'

DID YOU KNOW?

Miley's first premiere experience was for *Chicken Little* in October 2005. She really wanted to see the film so she managed to get tickets for herself and her mom. If you try to find a photo of Miley at the premiere, however, you won't have much luck. No one knew who she was so the photographers didn't bother asking her to pose for photos on the red carpet. It was a bit of a disappointing night for Miley because she had expected so much.

Miley decided to call time on *Hannah Montana* after the fourth season because she wanted a new adventure. Working on *LOL* had opened her eyes to what was possible. She wanted a break from the routine of working 8.30–6pm every day on the *Hannah Montana* set. Miley explained to *People* magazine at the time, 'I'm a little nervous because now it's like I don't have something to fall back on. But I'm getting excited. I think a lot of pressure is going to be taken off of me. I'm not going to be tied down to a company where they're like, "She sings! She acts!" I can choose when I want to do music and when to do movies. I won't have this mould they want me to fit into. I can just be what I want to be.'

Being in such a successful show had put a lot of pressure on Miley. There were days when she didn't want to go to work but had no choice because filming couldn't take place without her. She didn't like the fame it brought her or how commercialised everything was; she wasn't going to miss seeing her face on *Hannah Montana* duvet sets, lunchboxes and countless other items. Miley was no longer the naïve young girl who had auditioned for the show. As a seventeen-year-old she explained to *Parade Magazine*, 'I am not a doll, and people want to treat me that way. I'm older now. I have an opinion. I have my own taste.' She wanted the freedom to wear what she wanted every day, rather than what the wardrobe department picked out for her.

When she made the decision to quit *Hannah Montana*, it was not only the end of the road for Miley but for the other actors and actresses on the show. They all had to think about their futures and start auditioning for other roles. Billy Ray was obviously the first cast member to know. He supported Miley's decision 100 per cent and didn't try to change her mind. He revealed to *People* magazine at the time, 'I've gotten to go through this entire journey with Miley and watch her grow not only as a little girl to a young lady but as an actress. For any daddy out there to get to go through that with one of their children, it's an amazing journey.'

Miley's final Hannah Montana album was titled *Hannah Montana Forever* and was released on 15 October 2010. It was poorly received compared to her previous Hannah Montana albums, only managing to reach number 11 in the USA, number 21 in Ireland and number 38 in the UK.

Track Listing:
1. Gonna Get This
2. Que Sera
3. Ordinary Girl
4. Kiss It Goodbye

5. I'll Always Remember You
6. Need a Little Love
7. Are You Ready
8. Love That Lets Go
9. I'm Still Good
10. Been Here All Along
11. Barefoot Cinderella

For any actor or actress working on a Disney show there are lots of rules and standards that must be met. Disney is very protective of its young audience and wants stars to be positive role models at all times. Miley was very good at this but in November 2010 photographs of her drinking a Corona beer in Madrid appeared online and then, at her eighteenth birthday party, she was photographed looking very friendly with actor Avan Jogia. She was leaning backwards on some seating and Avan was virtually on top of her, with the press speculating that he was kissing her neck. Miley was dressed in a revealing black leather top and leather trousers, which lead to more negative comments in the press. She stayed at the party until 3am but to Smilers, this wasn't scandalous at all – Miley had just had an eighteenth birthday to remember.

Miley had been hoping for a chilled-out eighteenth and hadn't been planning on having a party. She told *OK! Magazine* beforehand, 'I hope I can just have a frickin' break… because I haven't had time, even a week to chill. So I'm probably just going to go to the beach or something. I'll take about ten of my friends with me and hang out with the people I never really get to see. A lot of my friends, they work, and I'm in the business too so I'll make sure we carve out some time so we can relax.'

Smilers really felt for Miley when, days after her birthday, a video of her smoking salvia (a herb which, although not illegal and believed by some to have healing properties, is also known as a hallucinogenic drug) with a bong surfaced. The world went crazy.

Miley had always been adamant in interviews that she would never smoke because of the damage it would do to her voice and throat but had obviously changed her mind and trying a legal high was a step further. The video was published by TMZ.com and showed her laughing hysterically and singing. She also lies down and thinks that one of the men with them looks like Liam, even though the person taking the video says he doesn't. She is encouraged to smoke again by her friend.

Billy Ray was shocked when he saw the video online and tweeted, 'Sorry guys. I had no idea. Just saw this stuff for the first time myself. Im so sad. There is much beyond my control right now.'

Miley admitted in an interview with *Marie Claire* a year after the incident that she should never have smoked from the bong. She explained that although other teens experiment with legal highs, she shouldn't have done so because 'they're not Miley Cyrus. They're not role models. So for me it was a bad decision, because of my fans and because of what I stand for.

'I'm not perfect... I made a mistake... I'm disappointed in myself for disappointing my fans.'

Miley told *Prestige* magazine at the time she thinks some

people look to her as a role model because she is so authentic. She said, 'If they [teenagers of the same age] tell you they haven't tried this or haven't experimented with that, they're lying. And I'll never do that because personally I can't, because there will be some proof on the Internet. It's weird... two complete extremes. I'm not some crazy lady who's gone off the deep end, because I definitely haven't. I just always try to be real. Every eighteen-year-old explores sexuality and experiments and tries things. You have to be true to yourself.'

She added, 'The [public] perception of my life is so different from who I really am. My dad is Native American, so I spend ninety per cent of my time outside, going on hikes. That's my lifestyle right now. The press seems to think that I'm trying to make this big turn and become a bad girl, really I'm trying to be more connected with the Earth, more connected with myself and figure out who I am, try to understand the world a little more.'

The final episode of *Hannah Montana* aired on 16 January 2011, just a few months after the bong scandal.

After all the drama died down a bit Miley got her fourth tattoo. It was a cross on the underside of her ring finger, to symbolise her love for Jesus. But she wasn't the first member of her family to express her faith in such a way as Trace and Brandi both have religious tattoos. The cross means a lot to her and, when she looks at it, she can remember everything that Jesus has done for her.

Miley also got a tiny line tattooed on her middle finger but she has never revealed what it symbolises. She got it changed to a peace sign a few months later.

When Miley attended the premiere of Justin Bieber's documentary film *Never Say Never* in Los Angeles on 9 February 2011, she couldn't help but offer him some advice. She explained to *Elle* magazine, 'I noticed he was taking all these photos of people and doing a lot of s**t, and I just grabbed him and said, "Just take a snapshot in your brain of this moment so you don't forget."

'I don't remember my *Hannah Montana* movie premiere and my 3D movie trumped everyone's at the box office. I don't remember being there. All I remember from that night is that I stopped and got a strawberry milkshake beforehand. That's all. It's crazy. You think you're in the present but you're not.'

Miley got her sixth tattoo during a trip to Venezuela in February 2011 – a huge Native American-style dream catcher on her right side. Because the dream catcher has four feathers it was rumoured to symbolise Trace, Brandi, Braison and Noah, and Miley's desire to keep them safe from harm.

DID YOU KNOW?
Trace has a dream-catcher tattoo on his neck.

When Miley left *Hannah Montana* behind her, she couldn't decide what to do next. She considered going to college and researched courses at New York University and in Savannah, Georgia, before deciding they weren't for her. She had thought that a move to New York might allow her to become a normal person for a while, something child/teen actresses Mary-Kate and Ashley Olsen had achieved after moving to the city to study fashion. Enrolling in a photography course was something that appealed to Miley, as she explained to *Rolling Stone* magazine: 'I love photography. I have a Canon 5D. I want to co-direct something soon. When they're saying, "Change this lens to this millimeter," I want to know what they're talking about.'

Miley wasn't ready for a normal life but she wasn't sure if she preferred singing or acting so vowed to continue doing both. She also decided that she didn't want to be typecast and wanted to try different types of acting roles. At the time she explained to the *Telegraph*, 'I'm kind of bipolar in my acting choices because I just want to do a little bit of everything. One day I'm telling my mom, you know, I want to do an action movie and then I want to be doing comedy and then all different types of things. I get a little bored so hopefully I'll get a chance to do a little bit of everything.'

DID YOU KNOW?

Miley gave some advice to budding actresses in a Q&A session with fans in *USA Today*. She said, 'Start taking singing lessons, acting lessons, dance lessons. When you're younger, get training, so when you are a little bit older and you can start going on auditions, you do have one-up on everyone. You should definitely go for it, but take your time and train.'

She had been living in her house for a year but Miley wanted a change and so decided to buy a second home, this time a bit further away from her parents. Her new $4-million house was in Studio City and had five bedrooms, seven bathrooms, a gym, a swimming pool and a spa. Rather than sell her first house, she decided to let her parents live there. However, Miley eventually decided that she didn't enjoy living in her new house so, when her parents decided to buy a villa two doors away from their old home, Miley decided that she and Liam should move back into the original house. She found it strange sleeping in her mum and dad's old bedroom at first but soon got used to it. Whenever Liam was away and she was feeling lonely, she could just nip across her neighbours' lawn and stay with her parents for a few nights.

CHAPTER TEN

FINDING MILEY

Rather than rush into releasing new music, Miley decided to take some time to chill out and figure out who she was away from *Hannah Montana*. She explained to *We Love Pop* magazine, 'Rather than going straight into work I was like, "You know what? I'm gonna buy a dope house and do whatever I want in it and become whoever I'm supposed to be within these next two years." For me it's like I've started from the bottom again but without the stress, I don't need to build this fan base, or make this money, or stress. I have the fans and the people are gonna watch so...'

During this period away from the limelight Billy Ray became concerned for Miley. She was no longer living under his roof and he couldn't protect her. He told *GQ* in February 2011, 'I'm scared for her. She's got a lot of people around her that's putting her in a great deal of danger. I know she's eighteen, but I still feel like as her daddy I'd like to try to help... at least get her out of danger. I want to get her sheltered from the storm. Stop the insanity just for a minute.'

At the time of the interview Billy Ray was living apart from his family as he had moved back to Tennessee in August 2010 after filing for divorce from Tish. He had found filming the final season on *Hannah Montana* traumatic as his home life was far from perfect. And he had decided against attending Miley's eighteenth birthday party in December because it was held in a bar and he knew that the press would jump on the fact that bars were supposed to be for people of twenty-one or over. If he went along, the press would say that he had endorsed it, he thought. He was sick of taking flack for Miley's handlers, who liked to keep things a secret from him and whom he thought were 'perhaps more interested in handling Miley's money than her safety and her career'. He admitted to *GQ* that he wished that she had never got the part of Hannah Montana because he blames the show for destroying his family.

When Miley read the interview, she was upset and for a while didn't speak to her dad. Billy Ray released an exclusive statement to *People* magazine in which he apologised for some of the explosive comments he had made while speaking to journalist Chris Heath at *GQ* magazine. He was going to fight to fix his family and in an interview on *The View* TV show in March 2011 he revealed that he and Tish were no longer getting a divorce. He said, 'I think for the first time me and my whole family are really communicating with each other. Things are really the best they've ever been.

'I love *Hannah Montana*. I love Disney. That didn't tear my family apart. Now fame, fame is a different animal, now fame you've got to be careful with that thing.'

When discussing the *GQ* interview, he said, 'I did learn this – doing an interview when you are mad and scared is a whole lot like going to the grocery store when you're hungry. It's not a good idea.'

He had been interviewed two weeks before Christmas and had been in a dark place.

DID YOU KNOW?

The press speculated that Miley and Liam Hemsworth were back together in March 2011 when they were seen hanging out again but no official statement was released. Miley's fans were thrilled when she and Liam walked the red carpet together at the *CNN Heroes: An All-Star Tribute* in Los Angeles on 11 December 2011. They were officially back dating!

In 2011 Miley embarked on her third tour. The Gypsy Heart Tour kicked off on 29 April 2011 and finished on 2 July 2011. She and her team decided against US dates and instead she performed in Australia, South America and Asia.

Miley decided to add another tattoo to her collection while on tour in Brazil. The tattoo artist Fabio Satori had turned up at her hotel thinking that he was going to be tattooing her crew after a friend of his called and asked him to come over. He explained to Brazilian magazine *EGO*, 'It was fun, it was a surprise on Sunday. A friend of mine works in the production of Miley and called me saying that the team wanted tattoos. Later, I was told that Miley wanted one as well and because, for her, leaving the hotel is always difficult, we did it at the hotel.'

While she was getting her tattoo Miley sang to Fabio, which made him feel very privileged. She had also explained to Tish why she was having the tattoo done. Fabio explained, 'Miley told her mother that she wanted something that refers to a safe port, something that reminded her that she always has a safe place to return to. The significance of the design is one of hope and a reminder to always have your feet on the ground.'

Shortly before she left for the Australian leg of the tour Miley hinted on the *Kyle and Jackie O Radio Show* that her relationship with Liam was back on. She said, 'I don't want to cross out the Australian boys but I may or may not be single... I love Australian boys though obviously.

'Liam and I are very close, I'm not going to comment too much, but you guys don't have to worry about that... I'm definitely not coming to Australia single.'

At the time Miley was very anti-Twitter and told the Australian radio hosts, 'I do not tweet, I do not social network, I try to stay out of it... for me, I complain enough about people knowing too much about my private life, so to go out there and exploit myself would be silly and hypocritical of what I stand for.'

Liam had visited her when she was touring Latin America but at first it was thought that he couldn't be there for her Australian dates because he was filming *The Hunger Games* in North Carolina. Miley's family were happy that the two of them had got back together, with Trace telling *Us Weekly*,

'We're homies... I support my sister in anything she does.' Billy Ray told E!, 'He's a great guy... He's solid. He's got great character.'

Billy Ray was excited for Liam because he just knew *The Hunger Games* was going to be massive and that, in playing Gale Hawthorne, Liam was going to show the world just how great an actor he is. He told the E! reporter Marc Malkin, 'Have you read that script?... The script is killer, and Liam is going to knock it out of the park. He's a tremendous talent.'

Neither Liam nor Miley said much to the media about getting back together because they wanted to keep things private. When Liam was asked by *Seventeen* magazine if they were back on, he replied, 'Who knows? Might be. The main thing is that we know how we feel. We know what's going on. It can get complicated bringing the rest of the world into it.'

But he did share in the interview what he does when he has relationship problems, saying, 'I like to put things on the table. I like when other people do that as well – you don't really get anywhere if you keep it all bottled up. You need to talk about it.'

Liam did actually manage to fly out to support Miley during a break in filming and his parents, Craig and Leonie, had front-row tickets for her Melbourne show. They wanted to show her how much they loved and supported her. When Miley found out they would be there, it made her feel nervous because of her sexy outfit for 'Can't Be Tamed'. Back then she found performing in front of people she knew quite intimidating. However, she was excited to be performing on stage again and also to meet her dedicated Smilers, who had made the tour a complete sell-out. She gushed to the BBC, 'One of the venues sold out – 60,000 tickets – in something crazy like an hour so the fans are really ready for it.'

In the run-up she fell sick but her fans sent her lots of encouraging messages, which helped her feel better. She even received messages from fans in the USA who would have loved to have seen her perform her Gypsy Heart Tour but weren't on her touring schedule this time around.

Miley's team had decided that it would be best if the tour only visited Australia, South America and Asia because her popularity in the USA had dipped after the controversy surrounding her eighteenth birthday. She herself explained to the *AP*, 'I just think right now America has gotten to a place where I don't know if they want me to tour or not. Right now I just want to go to the places where I am getting the most love and Australia and South America have done that for me.

'[I'm] kind of going to the places where I get the most love. I don't want to go anywhere where I don't feel completely comfortable with it.'

The Gypsy Heart Tour Set List:
1. Liberty Walk
2. Party in the USA
3. Kicking and Screaming
4. Robot
5. I Love Rock 'n' Roll/Cherry Bomb/Bad Reputation
6. Every Rose Has Its Thorn

7. Obsessed
8. Forgiveness and Love
9. Fly on the Wall
10. 7 Things
11. Scars
12. Smells Like Teen Spirit
13. Stay
14. Can't Be Tamed
15. Landslide
16. Take Me Along
17. The Driveway
18. The Climb
Encore
19. See You Again
20. My Heart Beats for Love
21. Who Owns My Heart

For this tour Miley wanted to shake things up a bit and do some covers that people wouldn't expect her to do so she picked songs that she and her brother Trace like to perform together when they're jamming in their mom's garage. She is a huge fan of Joan Jett so chose to do a medley of 'I Love Rock 'n' Roll', 'Cherry Bomb' and 'Bad Reputation'. In April 2011 she was honoured to perform a duet with Joan on the *Oprah Winfrey Show*. She revealed, 'It's amazing… I auditioned for my show [*Hannah Montana*] with "I Love Rock 'n' Roll," and the first album I ever made I had "I Love Rock 'n' Roll." So it's something that's always meant something to me. To see Joan stand up for chicks who want to play the guitar, [that's] something that's always inspired me, and I'm happy that I can be here with her.'

Performing a whole concert as herself rather than splitting between herself and Hannah wasn't difficult for Miley as it has always been a dream of hers. She added, 'Everyone likes making the transition real hard... Joan said, "You've got to do what you said, and you've got to be honest." It's not about how far I can push things so people will believe that I'm not Hannah Montana anymore. You just make the music that you love, and because I'm growing up, so does my music. It's not about making a statement.'

Another cover Miley chose to do was Fleetwood Mac's 'Landslide'. She is a huge Stevie Nicks' fan. Her Gypsy Heart Tour was about showcasing her great voice and not about how many different outfits she could change into. She revealed to Malaya.com.ph, 'The Gypsy Heart Tour is a dream-come-true. Not only because of all the beautiful cities I will get to visit, but also for all of the beautiful people I will get to meet... Gypsy Heart is not just a tour for me, but a mission to spread love.'

DID YOU KNOW?

Miley is also a huge Nirvana fan and her favourite Nirvana song is 'Heart Shaped Box'.

After her tour finished, Miley was asked by *Prestige* magazine whether she missed *Hannah Montana*. She replied,

No [laughs]. I miss the family vibe, but I don't miss the routine at all. I was so bored doing the same thing every day. It's a lot easier not being on a show, to live my life a little bit and do some of the other things that I want to do. I don't have to be back at a certain time. You're not worrying about a cast schedule or what the producers are going to think. I'm so grateful that I was able to be on that show, but even my little sister, who's 11, who wants to go into acting, I say, 'Just wait, dude.' Because the way you're going to be when you're my age and the way you are right now are so different. Don't put yourself into a situation where people are going to think of you as only one thing. You're going to change a lot. You're going to change every year. It interferes with your growing up if you're not strong and you're not sure who you want to be. I'm glad I'm not a character anymore and able to be me.

In July 2011 Miley decided to have two more tattoos on her hand. This time she chose to have 'karma' inked on her index finger. It was to be her first Indian-inspired tattoo. She also had an 'equals' sign inked on her ring finger. Later she tweeted a photo of the tattoo with the message 'All LOVE is equal'. Miley is a huge supporter of gay marriage and wanted to show the world how much she believed it should be legalised.

In one of her blog posts she wrote about how she feels. She said, 'Imagine finding someone you love more than anything in the world, who you would risk your life for but couldn't marry. And you couldn't have that special day the way your friends do – you know, wear the ring on your finger and have it mean the same thing as everybody else. Just put yourself in that person's shoes. It makes me feel sick to my stomach.'

She finished the blog by saying, 'We all should be tolerant of one another and embrace our differences. My dad [country singer Billy Ray Cyrus], who is a real man's man, lives on the farm and is as Southern and straight as they come. He loves my gay friends and even supports same-sex marriage. If my father can do it, anyone can.

'This is America, the nation of dreams. We're so proud of that. And yet certain people are excluded. It's just not right.'

In an interview with Bang Showbiz she confessed,

My favourite place to perform is London, because I have never seen more gay people in my whole life... When I go to London that's what it is. I feel like they are so much more open, much more than here in the US, where they're feeling trapped, where it's like, 'Can I even say I believe in gay marriage? Can I say that my favourite fans are my gay fans?' Am I allowed to say that, because half of America is still against it? It's like, I just feel like when I go to Europe, I feel very free with my fan base.

Miley had more tattoos that summer: she and Liam decided to have matching sugar-skull tattoos on their ankles. The sugar-skull symbol is normally associated with the Mexican holiday Day of the Dead. She had her second Indian-inspired tattoo when she had the 'OM' symbol tattooed on her left wrist.

In October 2011 Miley decided to visit Haiti to help the Starkey Hearing Foundation distribute hearing aids to over 400 deaf people. She was determined to do her bit, not because she needed publicity but because her heart aches for people in need.

For Miley the focus of the trip was on helping people so she didn't cake herself in make-up and her hair was roughly tied back in a bun. She wanted to blend in with everyone else there volunteering. Previously she had been to Haiti to help the foundation at the start of the year and had found it very moving. Miley told her fans, 'This second mission to Haiti was just as impactful to me as the first one. I grew up around music and couldn't imagine what it would be like for my siblings and me if we couldn't hear the magic of music.

'It's had such an influence on my life that I just want everyone to enjoy sound as it was intended.'

During her trip she bonded with lots of the children and made a special friend in a little boy called Emanuel. He loved cuddling her and Miley couldn't help but tweet a photo: 'That's a little boy named Emanuel :) we fit him w hearing aids... I've never seen a smile like his!

'I can't wait to go back.'

DID YOU KNOW?

After the terrible earthquake in January 2010, Miley had wanted to do something to help the people of Haiti. She put herself forward to sing on two charity singles: 'We Are the World 25 for Haiti' with another 80 big-name stars and 'Everybody Hurts' with mainly UK artists. Both singles went straight to the top of the music charts and raised a lot of money. Miley also organised an online auction on eBay to try and raise even more money. She auctioned off her dress from the Grammy Awards and two tickets to her *The Last Song* premiere and got other stars involved too. Britney Spears donated her dress from the 2008 MTV Video Music Awards and Nicole Richie gave some jewellery. There were so many stars who wanted to help.

Miley left her second trip to Haiti pleased that she had done a small thing to help those less fortunate than herself, but as well as receiving positive tweets from her Smilers, she received negative tweets from haters. They insulted her figure and said she was fat, which made her angry.

In retaliation she tweeted a photo of a woman suffering from anorexia with the message, 'By calling girls like me fat this is what you're doing to other people. i love MYSELF & if you could say the same you wouldn't be sitting on your computer trying to hurt others.'

Demi Lovato saw Miley's tweet and decided to show her some love, tweeting, 'Whoever called you that has it coming. Miss you more than ever.'

Miley replied, '@ddlovato AMEN! I will destroy any one that ever calls you the F word. You have the SEXIIIESTTTT curvyyyy body! I LOVE IT! #werkthosecurves.'

Miley really wanted to get the message across that girls should love their figures, writing, 'I don't wanna be shaped like a girl I LOVE being shaped like a WOMAN & trust me ladies your man wont mind either ;)'

Miley has always had to put up with people analysing the

way she looks but after she attended the CNN's Heroes 2011 awards the press were quick to say that she must have had a boob job because of her impressive cleavage. *Star* magazine even got three 'experts' to view photos of Miley on the red carpet in her yellow Roberto Cavalli gown and compare them with photos of the star at other events. Cosmetic physician Dr Tahl Humes of Vitahl Medical Aesthetics in Colorado told the magazine, 'Her breasts are very nice and round and it looks like she has had them done... If you look at the volume, it appears she has had a breast augmentation.'

Dr. Michael Niccole from CosmetiCare agreed, saying, 'It appears that Miley has recently undergone breast enhancement surgery.

'Push-up bras are great for cleavage, but don't help out a whole lot when it comes to the exterior breast volume, which is also what I notice in these photos.'

Finally, plastic surgeon Dr. Brian Glatt commented, 'Even a large weight gain would not produce breast enhancement to this degree without implants!'

The 'experts' might have agreed that Miley had had work done but she hadn't at all. She tweeted, 'Thank you for the compliment but these babies are all mine. I wish they'd realize you don't have to be fake to be beautiful!'

Miley's friends really wanted to make sure she had a special nineteenth birthday so Kelly Osbourne decided to throw her the best party ever. Despite being eight years older than Miley, the two stars had bonded on the set of their movie *So Undercover*. Kelly wanted the party to be really fun and allow Miley to let her hair down; the guest list was very select so that only people she trusted 100 per cent were there.

The party was held at the Beacher's Madhouse club in the Hollywood Roosevelt hotel. There were lots of performers, people dressed up and crazy things happening all the time. Afterwards Miley tweeted, 'Can't thank @MissKellyO for the best partyyyyy ever! =]]]] i loveeeee you! Let's just say there was a unicorn in the lobby!'

DID YOU KNOW?

Miley was feeling really ill that night so only came down from her hotel room at 2am but managed to party for a few hours. She apologised to her guests but no one minded; they were just sorry that she was ill.

Despite Kelly Osbourne only inviting Miley's closest friends, Miley was still betrayed when a video taken that night appeared online. For a joke she had been given a Bob Marley cake. She said, on receiving the cake, 'Thanks for waiting for three hours… and throwing a party. [Pointing at the cake] This is amazing. You know you're a stoner when your friends make you a Bob Marley cake. You know you smoke way too much f****** weed.'

Miley's representative released a statement, saying, 'It's all been taken out of context. The cake was a joke and Miley's response was intended to be sarcastic.'

Kelly was angry at the way things had been portrayed in the media, tweeting, 'let me make something very clear after @MileyCyrus salvia incident we started calling her bob miley as a JOKE!

'it makes me sick that @MileyCyrus so called "friends" would sell her out and lead people 2 believe she is someone that she is not!'

After Kelly posted the tweets supporting Miley she received lots of abuse. When Miley found out what was happening, she felt she had to step in and help. She wrote, 'Please stop bombarding my friends twitter pages with rude comments. NOTHING gives you the right to threaten people.

'I love u @MissKellyO :)'

Liam was furious too and told HollyScoop, 'She's in a room full of her best friends and you have one person who comes in there and videos it… The poor girl can't have one night where she can feel safe in her own world. It's ridiculous.' He also said, 'She's a happy, funny girl… she keeps me happy.'

But Miley didn't let the media's over-the-top reaction to her birthday party get her down and instead focused on doing more charity work. She wrote in her blog,

I'm proud to announce my participation in Amnesty International's latest music project, Chimes Of Freedom: The Songs Of Bob Dylan Honoring 50 Years of Amnesty International. I recorded 'You're Gonna Make Me Lonesome When You Go' for the collection, which will support Amnesty's life-saving human rights work.

Chimes of Freedom features over 80 musicians across the generational and musical spectrum who have donated their time to support Amnesty International through this beautiful project. [The] Album is dedicated to people worldwide who are unjustly imprisoned or threatened for the peaceful expression of their beliefs. & You can support Amnesty International's life-saving work by pre-ordering Chimes Of Freedom today!

Miley also attended the Sharing the Spirit Holiday Party for underprivileged children at the South Coast Plaza shopping centre in Los Angeles. December is a busy month for everybody but Miley made sure she kept 9 December free.

There were 450 children in attendance and Miley did her best to spend quality time with as many as she could. She added glittery eye shadow to some of the little girls, who were really excited to meet her. There was lots of dancing, good food to eat and a visit from Santa Claus. For the children, just staying up until midnight made the party magical. As they left, arms straining from the gift bags they were carrying, they couldn't believe they had met Miley Cyrus.

The party was the fifth of its kind and was organised by The Happiness Project, which works with children living without permanent homes in shelters and motels. Miley was thrilled to be involved and her family went along too. As well as meeting the children, she took time out to encourage the volunteers and applaud them for the work they do. She shared, 'What you get back for yourself is what you give out to other people.'

In many ways 2011 was a good year for Miley: she said goodbye to *Hannah Montana* and moved on with a new chapter of her life, she rekindled things with Liam and the future was looking bright after her Gypsy Heart Tour. She reflected how she felt as she ended the year in her Twitter biography, which was taken from The Smiths' track 'How Soon Is Now?': 'I am human and I need to be loved. Just like everybody else does.'

She advised her Smilers to focus on loving their friends and family, tweeting, 'I hope everyone has a merry xmas.

'2 make it more special try 2 spend every second w the ones u love & dont take their QT away by tweeting!

'BTW my bio is a song by The Smiths. One of my favourites You should check it out. Theres no trouble in paradise. I am so happy and SO LOVED.

'But it is true. I am HUMAN and I need to be loved. Just like all 4,108,281 of you. Its x-mas make sure everyone you love knows how much xx'

DID YOU KNOW?

Miley and Liam were voted Best Girlfriend–Best Boyfriend of 2011 in an online poll. Liam had been coming in third place but Miley encouraged her Smilers to get voting for him so he could beat Justin Bieber, Robert Pattinson, Brad Pitt and Ryan Reynolds to the top spot. She tweeted, 'Vote for Liam! He's not only the best boyfriend, he is one of the most incredible human beings I've ever known! It's been 2 1/2 years of pure bliss with him! Let's get him the #1 spot!'

Liam ended up receiving 35 per cent of the Best Boyfriend votes to secure the victory and Miley picked up a massive 45 per cent of the Best Girlfriend votes to win too.

CHAPTER ELEVEN
TAKING CONTROL

Miley was excited about celebrating Liam's twenty-second birthday on 13 January 2012. She tweeted, 'Got Liam the best bday pressie ever! Thank you for putting the cherry on top and making Liam's bday a TT [trending topic].'

Miley had bought Liam an English bulldog puppy, which they named Ziggy. Liam has loved dogs ever since he was a child and bulldogs are one of his favourite breeds. Miley and Liam might have shared their other dogs but Ziggy was officially Liam's.

A week later Miley threw a party for Liam at Club Icon, Los Angeles, so that he could celebrate with his nearest and dearest. He had been busy filming *The Hunger Games* in 2011 so it was a great opportunity for him to catch up with people he hadn't seen in a while.

Miley got Liam a penis-shaped cake for a joke and posed for some funny photos with it. The photos were later leaked and appeared online. But Miley is so used to things she does in private ending up in public that she is beyond caring sometimes; she has fun and knows that her family, friends and Smilers realise that. The photos weren't sexy, they were just silly and she didn't care about the negative stories that were written about the night: all that mattered was that Liam had a great time.

A few days after the party Miley sent a number of tweets showcasing how loved up she was feeling: 'Much needed chillllll pool day with my boooo. Thank you California for this lovely sunshine! Can't believe I'm laying out in January!

'If you have love, you don't need to have anything else. If you don't have it, it doesn't matter much what else you have.

'In my wildest dreams you always play my hero. In my darkest hours of the night you rescue me, you save my life.'

Miley loved showering Liam with kisses, even when the paparazzi were on the prowl because she wasn't going to let them ruin romantic dates out. She enjoyed sharing their relationship highs with Smilers online, writing on 30 January the lyrics from Augustana's track 'On the Other

Side' which described being with someone no matter what happens in the future.

As well as spending most of January loved up with her man, Miley found time to trick Khloe Kardashian, with the help of Kelly Osbourne, for an episode of *Punk'd*. Miley knew Khloe would find getting tricked hilarious and wouldn't be too mad with her.

She arranged a girls' night in at her house and when an actor pretending to be a pizza-delivery guy arrived, he asked to use Miley's bathroom. After shouting out in pain, the guy appeared with a prosthetic testicle stuck on his zip and it was down to poor Khloe to ring 911 and get some advice on what they should do.

Miley also punk'd Liam for her episode, which would air months later on 17 May. She had two 'naked people' climb inside her car while she went to get cash. They locked themselves in the car and poor Liam banged on the windows and tried his best to get them out but in the end the 'cops' arrived. They asked Liam if he knew the people after they insisted that they knew him. He got really angry at how ridiculous the situation was. Miley got him good and proper; he had no idea cameras were filming his every move. If you haven't seen it yet, check it out on YouTube by searching for 'Miley Cyrus Punk'd'.

Being punk'd by Miley was not something Liam ever

expected would happen, as he explained to Ellen DeGeneres: 'I knew she was doing the show... I thought she had enough respect for me not to do me.'

Liam nearly smashed the car's window trying to get the people out but he doesn't think he was too heavy-handed, considering the circumstances. He added, 'Your girlfriend comes running around and she's yelling hysterically... I think my instincts were right.'

Miley had also been planning on punking Justin Bieber with some skateboarders but she didn't realise that she was the one getting punk'd. Justin pretended to beat them up and Miley was left speechless as she watched things unfold.

DID YOU KNOW?

Miley is really clumsy and injures herself doing silly things. She once tried to do a front flip on her couch and ended up landing awkwardly and cracking her tailbone. Also, she broke her arm after tripping over a pillow.

Miley gained lots of new fans when she sang her version of Bob Dylan's 'You're Gonna Make Me Lonesome When You Go' on *The Ellen DeGeneres Show* on 6 February. The show was a tribute to Amnesty International and she was more than happy to be asked to perform her track from the *Chimes Of Freedom* charity album. Audiences in the studio and at home were touched by Miley's performance, with many comparing her to her legendary godmother Dolly Parton.

Dolly loves it when people compare Miley to her and

concentrate on how talented a singer Miley is, rather than the latest gossip surrounding her. She confessed to *Parade* magazine, 'I remember myself at her age. We've all been a bit too hard on her. I hope she holds it together because there's a world of things she can do. She should keep an eye on things and make wise decisions.'

Growing up, Miley listened a lot to the music of Etta James and Whitney Houston, so was shocked when they both passed away in early 2012 (Etta died on 20 January and Whitney died on 11 February). Miley had met Etta, who was a friend of Billy Ray's, lots of times. Her dad told Hollyscoop at the Grammy Awards, 'She's so sad about the loss of Whitney Houston... She was also very close with Etta James. Etta was a great influence to Miley. A lot of memories of me and Miley driving back and forth to the set of *Hannah Montana* with Etta James just roaring in the CD player.'

Miley decided to have 'Love Never Dies' tattooed on the bicep of her left arm after visiting Studio City Tattoos studio with Liam and some of their friends. The tattoo artist this time was a man called Illya, who had tattooed Miley before. A few weeks later she had a Nazar symbol inked on the index finger of her right hand. The Nazar symbol is from the Middle East and looks like an eye. Some cultures believe it wards off evil.

Miley really enjoyed attending *Vanity Fair*'s Oscars party on 26 February but hadn't been feeling at all happy beforehand. That day she had received lots of abuse from a hater, who had threatened to kill her. Miley wouldn't normally respond but felt she had to because she was so angry that someone would say such wicked things to her. She tweeted, 'I wont tolerate someone telling me 2 die.

'I think Twitter needs to take some responsibility and make it a safe environment!'

She even tweeted the person who had sent her the messages, asking him/her, 'U have nothing better 2 do than hate? That saddens me. Im surrounded by love Im sorry 4 whatever happened 2 make u so bitter.'

DID YOU KNOW?

Miley can't stop cleaning. She once tweeted, 'if i could change one thing about myself it would be my ocd. why do i never stop cleaning?! drives me nuts!'

Miley struggles to find genuine people who don't want to sell her out. Kelly Osbourne is one person she trusts completely and is one of Miley's best friends. The *Daily Telegraph* asked Miley what sort of qualities a best friend should have. She said, 'Honesty and trust... It's hard to find people you can trust. I probably only have four or five people who I would fully trust. You know, who would be there for me and tell the truth about me and to me.'

Because Miley is away travelling a lot, she can't always see her friends as often as she'd like. Thankfully, she's super-close to her mum and sisters so can always talk to them.

DID YOU KNOW?

Katy Perry is one of Miley's celebrity friends. When they shared a dressing room at the Grammys with Taylor Swift one year, Katy decided to do something

---

very strange. She explained at her iHeartRadio listening party, 'I asked them for a lock of their hair from each one of them, which is totally creepy, but awesome. I put little bows on them individually and put them in my purse. And that was my little secret and I'm a freak!'

Someone who Miley will always trust is her godmother, the Queen of Country Music Dolly Parton. She knew that Miley was super-talented when she was in *Hannah Montana* and told AOL Music at the time, 'That little Miley Cyrus... she's like a little Elvis! The kids love her because she's Hannah Montana, but what people don't realise about her is she is such a fantastic singer and songwriter. She writes songs like she's forty years old! She's really deep.'

In March Miley attended the LA premiere of *The Hunger Games* with Liam. It was the first time she had been in the supporting role, as normally Liam would be the one supporting her. She looked very sophisticated in a black bustier and maxiskirt by Pucci, complementing Liam, who was wearing a gorgeous Dolce & Gabbana suit. Miley didn't want to appear too short next to Liam so she wore her highest Christian Louboutin shoes to give herself a boost.

She told Ben Lyons from *Extra*: 'I'm a proud girlfriend; Liam's amazing in this. I think the characters... they all have so much depth. It's not a typical love triangle story and it's also really sad. I think the minute you start watching the movie you feel exactly where you are at that time.'

DID YOU KNOW?

Miley read *The Hunger Games* books after Liam secured the role because Noah recommended them to her. She explained, 'Liam started working on it and my sister was so excited that Liam was going to be in the movie. It's rare that you find a movie as good as the books, and I think this is going to live up to it and what everyone is so excited about.'

She might have acted alongside Liam in *The Last Song* but she was more than willing to let Jennifer Lawrence play his love interest Katniss Everdeen in *The Hunger Games* movies. Miley wanted to keep her personal life and working life separate.

DID YOU KNOW?

When Liam was preparing to play Gale, he received a text from his brother Chris, telling him, 'Hey, fatty, it's called Hunger Games, not Eating Games.' Chris had seen photos of Liam tucking into pizza and drinking beer when he should have been watching what he ate and drank.

Miley was pleased when *The Hunger Games* received amazing reviews from film critics and from fans of the books. It took $155 million on its opening weekend in the USA alone – more than double what the first *Twilight* movie managed to achieve. Liam's movie had the third biggest opening weekend ever in America!

Miley made sure that Liam knew how proud she was of him and his first pay cheque was framed and put on the wall of their house. He had had to work hard to become a successful actor, taking on other odd jobs just to get by (before he was in *The Last Song* with Miley he used to lay floors).

Miley knows what it is to work hard and is often left feeling drained and prone to sickness. When she was getting ready to perform at Muhammad Ali's seventieth birthday charity event on 24 March, she told Smilers that she was feeling under the weather. She tweeted two days before, 'Laying in bed sooooo sick :(send me positive energy! Gotta get healthy before celebrity fight night! Everything hurts.'

Thankfully, she was feeling much better on the day and managed to make it to the event, held at the JW Marriott Desert Ridge Resort & Spa in Las Vegas. Miley wasn't the only one performing that night, she was joined by Rita Wilson (Tom Hanks' wife), Rascal Flatts and Lionel Richie. They all wanted to raise as much money as possible for the Muhammad Ali Parkinson Center at the St Joseph's hospital in Phoenix.

Miley decided to wear two dresses at the event: a gorgeous orange dress with a split on the right-hand side showing off her toned and tanned legs on the red carpet and then a black-and-silver wrap dress for her actual performance.

She tweeted, 'Stoked for CelebFightNight) awesome to have JohnzoWest and Liam at my table here tonight.'

> **DID YOU KNOW?**
> Johnzo West joined Miley on stage and played the guitar and sang during her performance of 'You're Gonna Make Me Lonesome When You Go'.

Miley wore what looked to be a diamond ring on her ring finger at the event and had also tweeted a photo of her hand to show off some nail varnish but she insisted the ring definitely wasn't an engagement ring. She tweeted, 'I'm not engaged... I've worn this same ring on this finger since November! People just wanna find something to talk about! It's a topaz people!'

When Liam was interviewed by Jay Leno on 29 March, he confirmed that they weren't engaged but that they were 'in a happy relationship'. They were loving their life together with their dogs; they didn't feel like they had to get married or have kids just yet.

Miley echoed Liam in a series of tweets she sent to her followers that week. She wrote, 'woke up smiling & haven't stopped. feeling so much love, peace, and happiness around me.

'Happiness can only come from inside of you & is the result of your love for yourself. You are responsible for your happiness.

'If you take your happiness and put it in someone's hands, sooner or later, they will break it.

'3 dogs who love me unconditionally, a beautiful boyfriend, an amazing family, & 5.2m lovely followers.'

DID YOU KNOW?

For Miley, having a boyfriend who doesn't try to change her is really important. She wants someone to just be there to listen and support her rather than try to mould her into the type of girlfriend they want her to be.

CHAPTER TWELVE
UPS AND DOWNS

On 25 March 2012 Miley made history when she was named the first winner of the World Wish Day Star Award by the Make-A-Wish charity. She won the award for her exceptional contribution to helping the wishes of children with life-threatening medical conditions come true. The president and chief executive officer of Make-A-Wish America, David A. Williams, announced, 'For Make-A-Wish, celebrities are not simply promotional faces and voices – they are essential to fulfilling our wish-granting mission.

'This year we would like to honor a special celebrity who has gone above and beyond to create wish experiences that make life better for wish kids, families, and communities.'

DID YOU KNOW?

Miley has a desire to help people and, when she heard that seven-year-old Molly Dunne, who had pulmonary hypertension and HHT, wanted to meet her, she arranged a meeting in Miami. Miley spent time with her, wrote her a note and rang her up several times; she wanted Molly to know that she was there for her and even called her the night she passed away. She had been planning on calling in to see her that week but sadly it wasn't to be. Molly's family were so grateful to Miley for caring for Molly and in her last hours Molly was so happy to hear from her favourite singer.

Miley was a worthy winner of the the World Wish Day Star Award as she had granted wishes to over 150 children around the world and spent as much time with them as she possibly could. They always left her with big smiles on their faces as she treated them as if they were lifelong friends. She even granted the wishes of eight Make-A-Wish children when she went to collect her award at a special event in Phoenix.

But Miley went from feeling on top of the world to feeling extremely angry and insulted two days later when she found out that gossip blogger Perez Hilton had written a blog post entitled, 'Miley Cyrus Admits to Cutting??'

He wrote, 'We really hope it's not true, but pictures don't lie... and Miley Cyrus has been tweeting some red flags.

'All we want is for her to be happy and healthy, but we're not so sure that she's either anymore. People were super worried about her weight loss – which seems to be about 20 pound in a flash – before she cited a gluten allergy, and now she's tweeting things like this:

'"Scars remind us of where we've been. not where we're going."'

Perez knew that Miley's tweet was a quote but this didn't stop him writing the blog post or claiming that the faint lines on her arm on a zoomed-in photo were scars and 'look like cut marks'. Any Smiler looking at the same photo would think that the marks are simply from where Miley has worn a sweater or leant on something patterned. She would never self-harm and the whole blog post was based on speculation.

In the weeks that followed different gossip sites and newspapers wrote more negative stories, with *Celeb Dirty Laundry* even titling an article IS MILEY CYRUS NOW AN ANOREXIC WITH A NOSE RING? The *Daily Mail* wrote an article entitled REBEL WITHOUT A CAUSE: MILEY CYRUS WEARS A NOSE RING ON SUNSHINE STROLL WITH BOYFRIEND. In it they wrote, 'She already has numerous tattoos and now Miley Cyrus is continuing her show of rebellion with a new nose ring.'

Miley might have lost weight but she was far from anorexic and she got her nose pierced in 2009. She tweeted, 'How is a nose piercing I've had for 3 years a NEWs story. Don't get it.'

The anorexia rumours had started when she posted a photo of herself sniffing some takeaway with the message, 'Can't eat it so I'm just gonna smell the s*** out of it! My mouth is literally watering.'

Miley soon received lots of tweets asking if she had an

eating disorder so she quickly replied, 'For everyone calling me anorexic I have a gluten and lactose allergy. It's not about weight it's about health. Gluten is c**p anyway!'

Miley had simply changed her diet, eating a lot of chicken, fish, salad and fruit. She'd said goodbye to white bread and fried food too. Her Pilates classes were helping her tone up and Liam didn't have a problem with her being slightly slimmer.

The press might have been out to get Miley but she didn't care and just carried on with enjoying life. On Mother's Day she treated Tish to breakfast in bed before whisking her out for a lovely Mother's Day lunch. Tish loved Miley's gift to her, which was an expensive gold necklace. They had two reasons to celebrate, as it was Mother's Day and Tish's birthday too.

Miley had tweeted earlier in the day, 'Time to deliver breaky in bed with a side of jewelry to the hottest mama in town @tishcyrus.'

She also posted a photo of the two of them together with the message, 'Mama Tish LOVES her birthday/mommys day present.'

Tish was so happy that she couldn't help but tweet a message to her followers, saying, 'Had the most amazing Mothers Day/Birthday I have EVER had! Ive been so blessed with the most amazing kids and husband. Love them so much!'

DID YOU KNOW?
Miley might not have any children but she still gets a Mother's Day card from her dogs!

Miley has always vowed never to have a meaningless tattoo so Smilers were a bit confused when she had roman numerals that didn't make sense inked on her left arm. The numerals she chose were VIIXCI, which are the numbers 5, 1, 1, 10, 100 and 1. For the numerals to make any sense they would need spaces in between them. The month after Miley got the tattoo she was photographed coming out of a tattoo parlour with Trace and her roman numerals tattoo was bandaged up, leading people to speculate that she had been having it altered. It turns out the tattoo was supposed to be for 7/91 which is the month and year her parents met for the first time.

DID YOU KNOW?

Miley appears in the music video for her brother Trace's single 'Sippin on Sunshine'.

Miley knew she'd be slated by bloggers but she decided to be brave and daring when she picked her outfit for the Billboard Music Awards on 20 May 2012. She wore a pure white blazer by Jean Paul Gaultier with nothing underneath to the event at the MGM Grand Garden Arena in Las Vegas. The blazer showed off her ample cleavage and stopped at her butt cheeks. She accessorised with a chain necklace, a few rings and black-and-white striped peep-toe heels.

Miley was keen to be noticed on the red carpet and wanted to wear something sexy rather than cute. In the past she might have worn a floor-length gown but she was no longer a Disney princess: she was there to make a statement and present the Top New Artist Award to rapper Wiz Khalifa.

DID YOU KNOW?

Miley would go on to work with Wiz on his 2014 album *Blacc Hollywood*. When asked on *The Arsenio Hall Show* what Miley was like to work with he replied, 'Insane! But in a good way though, she's just a ball of energy. She smokes a ton.'

Liam might have been only twenty-two and Miley just nineteen but they knew they wanted to spend the rest of their lives together. However, Miley was shocked when Liam proposed on 31 May because she didn't expect it at all. The proposal was very sweet, with Liam asking Miley to marry him after she had sung her version of 'Lilac Wine' during one of her *Backyard Sessions* for MTV. She explained on *The Tonight Show With Jay Leno*, 'About twenty minutes after that song – that's one of Liam's favourite songs – he asked me to marry him, like, twenty minutes later so while I was singing that I had no idea and he's sitting there and I'm like, he's looking at me funny and then I know.'

They announced the news to fans and the media on 6 June, with Miley telling *People* magazine, 'I'm so happy to be engaged and look forward to a life of happiness with Liam.'

She sent a number of loved-up tweets when the news broke: 'I love you more today than yesterday but I love you less today than I will tomorrow.'

'life is beautiful.'

'thank you for all the love today :) I'm happy to share this news with you all. I feel like all my dreams are coming true. have a great day.'

Tish was overcome with emotion and tweeted, 'Wow! All of the love pouring out for Miley and Liam is incredible! So happy for my precious baby girl and the love of her life!'

Billy Ray shared her joy and tweeted, 'All I ever hoped for as a daddy was to see my kids reach their dreams. To find happiness, peace of mind, and someday know – true love.'

Her little bro Braison added, 'I wasn't gonna say anything. But I am so happy for @MileyCyrus. Never thought any man would be good enough but I know he makes her happy.'

One of her friends from childhood, Lesley Patterson, wanted to wish them well and tweeted, 'Congrats @MileyCyrus on your engagement!!!! So happy for you and Liam! Miss y'all!'

Miley's engagement ring was designed by Neil Lane, who had been commissioned by Liam to create a unique ring that was both romantic and beautiful. The diamond he chose was handcut at the end of the nineteenth century. Liam absolutely loved the ring and tweeted a photo of it with the message, 'Thank you all for the support. We are both very happy!'

Miley chatted to journalist Laurie Sandell from *Marie Claire* about how perfect the ring was. She admitted, 'We'd been kind of talking about [getting engaged], and I saw something like it online at one point and thought it was really pretty, but I usually wear rose gold. I just love that it's old and has a story. And I'm happy because it doesn't look like anything else I wear.'

DID YOU KNOW?

Adam Shankman, who was one of the producers on *The Last Song*, cried when he found out that Miley and Liam were engaged. He told *People* magazine, 'It's extraordinary, and I'm so happy... I'm scared at how beautiful those children are going to be.'

Miley chatted to TV host Ellen DeGeneres about her wedding day, saying,

That moment when he first gets to see me in my dress and everything all together, it has to be perfect. It has to be like a soundtrack in a movie. That's the one day that movie crap is real. That romance. That look is the time that you get that. I've been to probably ten, twenty weddings and I've seen that real look five, six times. It's rare that people just stop to really look the person in the eye and know that this is your life together.

There is some rumour going around that I'm having, like, forty-seven weddings. I'm not. I'm having one wedding. That's my day and whatever I want on that day will be about me and that moment.

Less than two weeks after getting engaged Miley and Liam were forced to live separately for a while because Liam needed to be in New Orleans to film his movie *Empire State* and Miley was working away from home too. Miley found being on her own really hard going and tweeted Smilers to let them know how she was feeling. She wrote, 'I miss my mommy & my fiance #homesick.'

Because they were apart rumours started, saying they were having problems. Miley decided to tweet a message to her mum that all her followers could see. She wrote, '@tishcyrus I love my fiance and he loves me. All the rest is bull s**t. We get to live a life of happiness no one can take that away from us.'

Miley had simply been having fun with her best friend Cheyne Thomas in Miami and the paparazzi had taken photos and sold them to newspapers and magazines around the world. But Miley had been working hard in the studio on her new album and just needed a break. She didn't appreciate the *Daily Mail* writing a story entitled LOOK AWAY NOW LIAM! NEWLY ENGAGED MILEY CYRUS GETS VERY CLOSE TO HER MALE FRIEND AS THEY FROLIC IN THE POOL.

Miley tweeted, 'so now because I am engaged I can't have a friend of the opposite sex? Can't have a friend help me out while I'm working alllll day?

'maybe YOU would have friends too if you'd get your face out the tabloids & start living your own life ? unfortunate.'

Cheyne tweeted, 'Not sure if u guys realize it or not but you can hang out with ur friend and look happy and be having fun... there's nothing wrong with that...

'If it seems strange behavior to you then maybe u should reevaluate your friendships and quit worrying about mine.

'People should learn to be happy for others and not always try to ruin everything they're happy as hell let them have that.'

Miley, Tish and Cheyne were furious about what had been written about an innocent swim. Tish tweeted, 'So sad that the nasty tabloids have to make up stories to sell their trashy mags. Cant they just leave these 2 alone and let them be happy?'

DID YOU KNOW?

Cheyne was working in Starbucks before Miley told him that she wanted him to be her personal assistant. He had been her friend for years and she knew he was someone she could trust.

Miley was at Liam's side at the first ever Australians in Film Awards, which were held at the InterContinental Hotel in Century City, Los Angeles on 27 June 2012. For the occasion she decided to wear a little black dress designed by Australian design house Zimmerman. She decided on black because it would let her blend in a lot more and wouldn't take the media's focus away from Liam. The whole evening was held in honour of her man, actress Yvonne Strahovski, director John Polson and studio executive Harvey Weinstein.

While she was there Miley was interviewed by *People* magazine and told them, '[Australians are] way hotter [than American guys]. There's no competition. I think there's a masculinity about [Australian guys] that is probably like growing up in the South, like what I did. They are a little bit more respectful, I suppose.'

When the Australians in Film President Andrew Warne announced that Liam was the winner of the Breakthrough Award, Miley was so proud. Andrew told the audience of

300, 'We are delighted to honour Liam Hemsworth with the 2012 Breakthrough Award. The string of his recent and upcoming films demonstrates an undeniable star power. From *The Expendables 2* opposite Sylvester Stallone and *Paranoia* opposite screen legends Gary Oldman and Harrison Ford, to *Arabian Nights* with Dwayne Johnson and Sir Anthony Hopkins, we believe this is only the beginning for Liam Hemsworth.'

When Liam went on stage to give his acceptance speech, he made sure to mention how he met Miley, saying of his *Last Song* audition, 'I was fortunate enough to get called back in and read with my now fiancée and we read together and fell in love and got married... Well, not married yet.'

Miley shouted out, 'We will be!' which was then repeated by a smiling Chris.

The two of them had a great night but the next day Liam had to fly back out to New Orleans to carry on filming *Empire State*. Miley was gutted and tweeted, 'The weight of the world is too strong. The wait to be yours is too long. In this bed alone I feel too small. I want none if not all.'

DID YOU KNOW?

Liam finds Miley really sexy when she dribbles. He revealed to *Who* magazine in November 2011, 'There is this place in Nashville called Steak and Shake, which is pretty much the best food, ever. That is our secret, sexy place to go... When I look over at her when she's biting into a steak sandwich and there is some steak sauce dripping down her chin, there is nothing sexier than that.'

In July Liam was busy filming another movie, *Paranoia*, in Philadelphia. Miley decided to visit him with their dog Ziggy, but when they tried to do simple things like walk down a street together, they couldn't without getting followed by dozens of paparazzi.

Being stalked on a daily basis really irritates Miley because she wants to be able to have a normal life. She vented her anger in a number of tweets: 'How is it legal for men I've never seen before to sit in front of my house and then follow me around! So shady and scary.'

'I hate paparazzi with a passion. disgusting pigs. (no offense to pigs).'

'Why do paparazzi feel the need to video me walking Ziggy? I mean really? Are headlines really gonna read Mileys dog takes a sh*t?'

'thinking about eating Ziggy's dog food I'm so hungry. But I'm stuck in this hotel like friggen Rapunzel cuz of the soul suckers on the street.'

After talking about it, Miley and Liam decided to get another tattoo together. This time they chose to have lines from a speech President Franklin D. Roosevelt gave in 1910 inked on their arms. Liam had the first part: 'If he fails, at least fails while daring greatly.' Miley's tattoo continues, 'so that his place shall never be with those cold and timid souls who neither know victory nor defeat.'

Miley choose the inspirational quote because, as she explained to *Rolling Stone*, it is about 'how people judge who wins and who loses, but they're not the ones in there fighting... It's about critics.'

July seemed to be a rough month for the star as she sent

a few tweets that made Smilers wonder if the bloggers were right about Miley and Liam's relationship being in trouble. She wrote on 8 July, 'Maybe you could've been something I'd be good at.'

And two days later, 'do you not think that far ahead? Cause I've been thinkin bout forever.'

Miley debuted a new blonde razor-cut bob and for a while it seemed to lift her mood. She shared a photo of her new look with her followers with the message, 'Now that I'm blonde I gotta give duck lips in every photo.'

She also tried to get some free Chanel handbags and accessories by tweeting a photo of herself with a Chanel bag and the message, 'Yo! Chanel hook a sista up!!! Loveee.'

When she saw that Chanel had made a skateboard, she knew she had to have one and tweeted, 'I just wanna skateboard...

'soooo I really need a custom @chanel skateboard! Aint that right @Pharrell.'

Getting tattoos always seems to make her happy and she decided to get another finger tattoo, this time in red font. Her 'BAD' tattoo is thought to be a tribute to Michael Jackson as *Bad* is the name of his seventh album, which was released in August 1987. Miley is a huge Michael Jackson fan and when he died, she tweeted, 'Michael Jackson was my inspiration. Love and blessings.'

In a 2010 interview with MTV she said,

He was a baby when he started in the industry. And it's hard, you gotta be strong. It's so crazy with the media and all that. Nobody ever wrote an article just to say,

'Hey, Michael, we really appreciate what you do.' I wish I would have had the opportunity. I wish I would have known. I wish I would have had some kind of determination to be like 'How can I get in touch with Michael Jackson and let him know how much he means to me?' Because not enough people told him, and I think it's sad that he had to wait until it's too late to tell people what he did. But I think he knows.

Miley decided to put Liam first and visited him when she should have been at the Teen Choice Awards at the Gibson Amphitheatre in Los Angeles on 22 July. She had won the Choice Female Hottie Award and the Choice Female Fashion Icon Award. Missing the show was a big deal for Miley because she loves going every year. She tweeted, 'So sad I [wasn't] able to be at TCA tonight! My fans are amazing! Thank you beyond! TCA is my favorite cause it comes from y'all :) I love u.'

She joked around with her Smilers in August when she tweeted a photo of two naked women just wearing body paint. The faces of the women were hidden so many thought that it could be Miley and her back-up dancer friend Jen Novak. In the photo the women are opposite each other with faces painted on their bodies. One woman is standing upright and the other one is doing a handstand. The artist who painted them was very talented as at first glance you just notice the cartoon faces. It is only when you study them that you realise they are painted on naked women.

Cheyne Thomas tagged Miley and Jen in the photo but

Miley didn't reveal if it was of them, only writing, 'our love is our greatest art.'

Jen tweeted, 'After today... i have a whole new appreciation for this pic;)'

Miley replied, 'Cause were breasttttt friends.'

Miley insisted that she and Liam weren't the jealous type because they trusted each other completely. She told *Marie Claire*, 'People will say, "Oh Liam is so close to Jennifer Lawrence [from *The Hunger Games*]." Well yeah, they just shot a movie together! He's supposed to ignore her because she's a chick?

'I could be standing next to a guy who is wearing a rainbow-colored shirt that says "I'm gay" and people would still write, "Who is that guy with Miley?" It's all bulls***. Luckily, neither one of us is super-jealous. We know each other and would never do anything to hurt each other.'

Miley and Liam set themselves boundaries and turned down scripts that they felt might upset the other person. Being engaged made her feel more secure when Liam had on-screen romances because she knew that he would be coming home to her. She admits that, if they were just girlfriend and boyfriend, she might have felt differently.

DID YOU KNOW?

Once when Miley was out of town, her home was surrounded by a swat team after someone made a prank call to say that someone was trying to kidnap her and there had been a shooting.

In August Miley revealed a secret to her Smilers: she had been the female vocalist on a track by Israeli DJ Borgore. 'Decisions' had been released two months earlier but received a huge surge in sales once Smilers found out about it. Borgore was delighted because he had no idea that she was going to reveal all. He told *Rolling Stone*, 'What we were trying to do is make a tune together that we're super-happy about and just see people's real opinion about this.

'If someone used to like the tune before he knew she was on it, and now he doesn't like it just because she's on it, he's lying to himself... I think being nonconformist is being the biggest conformist.'

DID YOU KNOW?

Borgore had no idea that Miley was a big star because he had never seen *Hannah Montana* before but he wanted her to be on the track because he thought she had such a good voice.

CHAPTER THIRTEEN

HAPPY, PRETTY, FREE

Miley was ready for a dramatic change and decided that her hair needed the chop. She wanted to share everything with her followers so posted up 'before' and 'after' photos of her hair being cut and styled by celebrity stylist Chris McMillan. Before her stylist got to work she tweeted, 'If you don't have something nice to say don't say anything at all. my hair is attached to my head no one else's and it's going bye bye.'

On two of the photos she pulls a shocked face as Chris stands behind her, holding scissors to her bun. After revealing her new look Miley received some abusive messages, saying her new style was horrible. She quickly responded with the message, 'My dad Billy Ray Cyrus used to tell me opinions are like ass holes everybody has one. Love my hair feel so happy, pretty, and free.'

Miley also revealed what Liam thought of her new style, tweeting, 'He loves [my haircut]. Last night he said I look the happiest he's seen me in a while :) he likes seeing my eyes more.'

DID YOU KNOW?

Miley had actually wanted to cut her hair super-short for many years. She confessed to News.com.au, 'I've wanted to cut my hair forever, since probably like six years ago we did an episode where they made my hair look like Twiggy. Ever since I saw that I wanted to do it, but it was just getting the guts to finally take a razor and know that your hair does not grow back overnight. It's not the cutting it that scares you, it's the growing it out.

'It's so worth it, I could never see myself with long, long hair again, it just seems like so much maintenance. This is so easy, so nice.'

Less than two weeks after her change in hairstyle Miley sent some cryptic messages on Twitter. She wrote, 'Love is a battle, love is a war; love is growing up.

'To love is to suffer. To avoid suffering one must not love. But then one suffers from not loving.'

Fans knew that Miley and Liam wanted a long engagement but they just hoped things were OK. Miley seemed fine at the MTV VMAs on 6 September 2012 when she was one of the presenters. Wearing a gorgeous black silk Emilio Pucci gown, she welcomed Pink onto the stage to perform her songs 'Get The Party Started' and 'Blow Me

One Last Kiss'. Miley told the audience, 'The artist who is about to take to the stage inspired artists like me to be true to ourselves, sing from the heart and be individuals.' Lots of people compared Miley's hair to Pink's hair but Miley didn't care, tweeting afterwards, 'Woahh 2 girls have blonde short hair! The whole world should go in to panic mode. Redickkkk.'

DID YOU KNOW?

After Miley had her hair cut some people tried to insult her by saying that she looked like a lesbian. She told the *Toronto Sun*, 'Everyone said I was a lesbian but I'm like, "Being a lesbian isn't a bad thing. So if you think I look like I'm a lesbian, I'm not offended. You can call me much worse." I've been called much worse. Being a lesbian is a compliment more than what else they call me.'

On the red carpet journalists kept asking Miley about her new hair. She told *Access* magazine that it is much easier to manage and she loves that her hair doesn't cover her face anymore. She used to wear it in a bun all the time because she didn't want to have to deal with it so the new look was much better for her. Miley really wanted to get across that she was going to be releasing new music and she'd just relaunched her website. She said, '[I'm] just kind of showing everyone what direction I'm going into. I'm really happy. I think I've finally found out who I am, and it changes every freaking day, as you can tell. Every time I write a song, I feel like I can finally be me, because I'm not stuck into a label, all of these people telling me who to be. I get to write and work with amazing producers. It's really fun!'

Noah attended the awards with Miley because she was desperate to meet One Direction. She wanted Miley to introduce her but instead her sister let her have her all-access pass. Katy Perry was actually the one who ended up introducing Noah to Harry, Niall, Zayn, Liam and Louis.

DID YOU KNOW?

Miley once agreed to appear on *Good Morning America* just for Noah. Justin Bieber was on the show that day and Noah was desperate to meet him face to face.

Smilers were blown away when MTV screened Miley's *Backyard Sessions* in early September. They had been recorded in the summer and showed a relaxed Miley singing with her band in her garden. It was after one of these sessions, of course, that Liam had proposed.

Miley did a great cover of the classic James Shelton's song 'Lilac Wine', despite it being a hard song to sing. She made it look so easy that some people doubted that it was 100 per cent her and left nasty comments underneath the video on YouTube. Miley's keyboard player Mike Schmid told super-fan Jackie (@MileyLiamLOVE),

I don't get involved with tabloid BS because it's none of my business. But when people say Miley is untalented or can't sing, that's something I DO know about, because I've been working with her since she was 14 and the girl is REALLY good. She knows what she's doing, and she does it with more style and personality than most people ever could. So yeah, it does bother me when people say that we 'fixed' up her vocal.

I recorded it with her, and all you're hearing is our live take, with some compression and a little reverb on the vocal to give it spice (which is VERY standard). There WERE no producers. We just played it, then our buddy Hager mixed it and added said compression and verb. What you hear is pretty much what it sounded like in the yard. That IS the real Miley.

Most celebrities have to deal with some fans that go to extremes and Miley is no exception. On Saturday, 8 September a man called Jason Luis Rivera was caught in the front garden of her home at 4.10am, carrying some scissors. He told the cops who arrested him that he was Miley's husband. Thankfully, she wasn't at home so wasn't harmed.

After appearing in court, Rivera was sentenced to 18 months in prison and was told that he is not allowed to be within 1,000 yards of Miley at any time. She needed a permanent restraining order against him just in case he tried to see her again after being released.

Miley might have put her acting career on hold to concentrate on her music but when she was invited to appear on the CBS hit comedy *Two and a Half Men*, she couldn't say no – it was too good an opportunity to pass up. The show's executive producer Jim Patterson spoke to Yahoo TV about how excited they were to have her work on the show. He said,

We approached her. Ashton and she are friendly, and actually Angus appeared on her show two years ago, I think it was. I think Jon Cryer actually appeared on her show as well. And her character on *Hannah Montana* was obsessed with Ashton... She kind of knew everyone a little bit.

She's on for two episodes right now and if things turn out well and she has fun, we'd love to have her back... We think it's going to be a great dynamic. She'll play a romantic interest for Jake [played by Angus T. Jones] and he's never really had that. This is going to be his first real relationship kind of thing. He's no longer the half man on the show. He's... in the Army, gonna have a girlfriend, experience love and heartbreak and all that kind of stuff.

After shooting her scenes Miley tweeted, 'I had the best time on 2.5 men 2 episodes down :) I see why they've done 10 years of this. Such an awesome group of people.'

Miley had some great lines on the show, including, 'Hi, I'm Missi! Everyone thinks it's short for Melissa but it's actually for Mississippi – the river, not the state, because according to my parents, I was conceived on the deck of a gambling boat when my daddy won a $5,000 jackpot.'

[When she wants to sunbathe topless] 'Do you mind if I pop the girls out? You know, get a little colour on Kim and Khloé.'

[Trying to encourage Walden to date her mom] 'If it helps at all, she actually just had her boobs done. They actually used mine as a model. The doctor even put them in his catalogue.'

Tish loves watching Miley take on a new challenge and on 1 October she wrote on her blog, 'Today was such an amazing day! I love going to watch Miley work. She makes me so proud and sometimes I can't believe we are really living this crazy life. I feel extremely blessed! Miley really is incredible to watch when she's working on something she loves. The one thing about Miley is when she loves, she loves deeply, when she's working, she is giving 110 per cent. She has so much passion for life and I love that so much about her.'

DID YOU KNOW?

Later that day Miley, Liam and the rest of the Cyrus family went to see Brandi's band Frank + Derol perform a concert as part of the Wolfgang Tour. No matter how busy Miley is, she will always try to support her siblings whenever she can. She shared a photo of the venue and Trace tweeted, 'My sister Brandi killed it at her show tonight! So proud of her for going on this tour! 1st show was sold out! Good sign!'

Miley's first *Two and a Half Men* episode, 'You Know What The Lollipop Is For', aired in the US on Thursday, 18 October at 8.30pm. Her second episode, 'Avoid the Chinese Mustard', aired on Thursday, 8 November. Miley's episodes had some of the highest ratings of the season.

Her co-star Angus T. Jones, who plays Jake, thought that Miley was a great guest star and he would love to work with her again. He told *E! News*, 'She is extremely talented, extremely hilarious and she's an awesome person to have on set.'

He maintained that he doesn't have a crush on her and revealed that he found their kiss together weird: 'It was silly. Acting kissing is one of the weirdest things that you have to do.'

CHAPTER FOURTEEN

BROKEN-HEARTED

Miley has always struggled to keep her private life private on Twitter so when she tweeted, 'Why do I torture myself and what ps I love you. ahhhhhh. I have got to pull it together,' fans thought it was a public apology to Liam. According to *HollywoodLife*, he had been unhappy with some of the tweets she'd been sending; tweets like 'Thought of the day: maybe it's not that they love you less, they just love you the most they are capable of loving', 'sometimes i feel like i love everyone more than they love me. hatttte that feeling', 'Ever feel like you want just... something more. Not sure what exactly... passion perhaps.'

The press might have been suggesting that Liam was growing tired of Miley but they both appeared in the video for Borgore's 'Decisions'. It was filmed at Beacher's

Madhouse in Los Angeles, the place where Miley had her nineteenth birthday party. In the video a wild party is going on and, after Miley appears out of a cake and a whole lot of crazy antics take place, the two of them make out, with Liam wearing a unicorn mask. It was all very surreal and off the wall.

On 11 October 2012 Miley's former boyfriend Nick Jonas performed a new song called 'Wedding Bells at Radio City' in New York. The lyrics strongly suggested that Nick was still in love with Miley and before he started singing he told the crowd, 'Some things happened in this past year that affected me a certain way in that moment and I had to go write a song about it in that moment and, although it's not the way I feel at this moment in time, hopefully this gives you a glimpse into what that experience was like for me.

'It's an incredible thing and it should be valued when you appreciate someone and care for someone and there is history. But as you move on in your life and move into maturity, you have to take the experience with you as memories and not your reality. This song is called "Wedding Bells".'

DID YOU KNOW?

In the song Nick sings, 'If you recall our anniversary falls eleven nights in June.' His and Miley's anniversary was 11 June.

Miley was asked whether she thought the song was about her a week later when she was interviewed on Ryan Seacrest's radio show. She replied, 'I don't know who else is getting married… so I feel like that's pretty blatant, it's whatever. Like I said, everyone has to write songs that are about things that they felt and he even introduced that this isn't the way that I am. So you can't ever hate on someone for writing about something you've been through. I think that you kind of get a fair warning when you date an artist and someone that's a writer, when you're going through things, that you're going to end up hearing about it on the radio.'

For Miley's twentieth birthday, on 23 November 2012, animal-rights campaigners PETA decided to give her an unusual gift: they sponsored a rescue pig called Nora. PETA executive vice president Tracy Reiman explained in a press release, 'PETA knew that sponsoring a rescued pig was the perfect birthday present for a young woman who spends so much time encouraging others to help animals. From promoting animal adoption to speaking up for cows who suffer on dairy farms, Miley never stops letting her millions of fans know what they can do to make the world a kinder place.'

Her Smilers decided to donate to two charities in Miley's honour and she was truly touched. The charities they chose were the Starkey Hearing Foundation and the Saving SPOT! Dog Rescue. Miley tweeted, 'So much BIRFFFDAY love!… I wish everyday was like this :).

'Thank you to all my fans who donated to @starkeyhearing @spotrescuedogs for my birthday :) y'all topped it again best bday present by far!'

DID YOU KNOW?

Miley had tweeted a cheeky message two days before her birthday, saying, 'If I don't get at least one big booty hoe my friends are officially not my friends anymore.'

The day after her birthday she shared a photo of herself jumping on a cushion with two balloons – one shaped as a '2' and one shaped as a '0' – behind her. She tweeted, 'Great night last night. Thanks to everyone who celebrated with me. & yes I did get a big booty hoe 4 my birfday.'

Miley decided to add to her pack by rescuing a new puppy and went with Noah to choose the puppy, whom she named Penny Lane. She posted a picture up on Twitter to show Smilers just how tiny she was compared to her other dog Sophie and another photo of herself giving Penny a big kiss. She tweeted, 'I love Penny Lane ❤ #rescueislove @SpotRescueDogs.'

DID YOU KNOW?

Penny Lane actually became Noah's dog more than Miley's.

Miley was so excited about the new music she was recording that she told Smilers she would be releasing something by the end of 2012 but it wasn't to be. Fans were really disappointed because they'd been waiting ever since *Can't Be Tamed* came out two years earlier. The delay was partly due to Miley moving labels, from Hollywood Records to RCA Records.

When a fan tweeted to ask whether she was going to

release something, she responded by tweeting, 'Folks! When you write your music and your creating it doesn't happen overnight or on a deadline. You write til your heart is empty then you live your life til you have stories to tell again and then you make ANOTHER record.'

Miley was devastated when her two-year-old dog Lila died in December. She tweeted, 'Can't think of one good reason to get out of bed today.'

Later she explained why she was feeling so down: 'For everyone asking... I have never been so hurt in my life. My heart has never been so broken... Lila my sweet baby girl has passed away.

'Broken. Gonna go MIA for a bit. Need some healing time. Thank you to everyone who has sent love my way. I need it.'

Her mum decided that she needed to share with fans what happened and wrote on her blog a few days later,

As for Miley, it's been a really tough week. As you all know her beloved baby girl Lila passed away. Everyone has been so precious and so supportive of her and I love you all so much for that. Miley loved Lila more than anyone can imagine.

The way that Lila was taken from her was beyond terrible. Sometimes things happen that we just can't understand. Miley still isn't ready to talk about it, but I thought you guys should know what happened.

For some unknown reason, Ziggy grabbed Lila. Not really sure if she was playing or what? She grabbed her in just the wrong spot and Lila didn't survive.

Please understand that Miley isn't ready to talk about
this and we don't think Ziggy is a mean dog.

Miley and Liam made the hard decision to get Ziggy
rehomed. They took her to SPOT! Dog Rescue and the new
home they found had no children or pets. Although they
knew that Ziggy going to a new home was for the best, they
still found it hard because they loved her so much.

Miley was so upset that she struggled to stay positive but
having her other dogs close by helped her feel better. She
shared a photo of herself hugging and kissing her dogs with
the message, 'This is just what mommy needed. These
precious babies still here on earth are just what the doctor
ordered. #pupsheal.'

She also added another photo of Mary Jane sat on her
knee, tweeting, 'Mary Jane is trying to sit on my lap the way
Lil Lila used to. It's workin out a lil differently.
#feelsgoodtosmile.' Her knees must have been aching after-
wards because Mary Jane is a big dog.

By the time Christmas came around Miley seemed back to
normal, which was a huge relief to her Smilers, who didn't
want her to spend the holiday time miserable. On 23
December she tweeted a very cheeky photo of herself giving
the thumbs up, with a naked blow-up doll sat next to her in
her car. Her message read, 'Does this count for the carpool
lane? Such a nice Xmas gift.'

She also tweeted, 'Just played guitar for 3 hours straight
without realizing it,' and a photo of herself by a roaring fire
with the message, 'The weather outside is frightful... But the
fire is soooo delightful. Let it snow, let it snow, let it snooooow.'

On 28 December she shared a photo of Floyd, Mary Jane and Happy sat on a huge couch with her followers. She wrote, 'My Family... all i can think about is puppies. i think i have OWDD (obsessed with dogs disorder).'

Miley was soon visiting SPOT! Dog Rescue again and found a new puppy to adopt. She tweeted a photo of her new addition with the message, 'Meet Bean... Bean is a little girl. She is a chihuahua mix of some type :) she brought so much sunshine!!! I love my little bean so much.'

She nicknamed her 'my little burrito' in one photo and fans were quick to tweet how cute she was. Miley warned them, 'Unfollow me if you don't want 100000 photos of Bean.'

DID YOU KNOW?

Miley's friend Cheyne caught Miley asleep in her dogs' house cuddling Bean and Floyd and couldn't help but take a photo and share it on Twitter. Miley didn't mind at all.

Even though she had Bean and her other dogs, Miley still missed Lila loads, sharing a photo of the two of them together with the message, 'I miss u every second of every day.' And then later, 'I haven't been the same since you left and I don't know if I ever will be.'

CHAPTER FIFTEEN
FRESH START

Miley was really busy in January 2013 promoting the movie *So Undercover*, which she had filmed alongside Kelly Osbourne in December 2010. They finished filming a month later but some extra scenes needed to be reshot in August 2011. It must have been strange for Miley to have to promote something she had done while doing *Hannah Montana* because her whole life had changed so much since then. The film was released straight to DVD in the USA on 5 February 2013. This disappointed lots of Smilers, who had thought it would be shown in cinemas first.

Miley played a character called Molly Morris. She is a private investigator who is hired by the FBI to go undercover in a college sorority. Her job is to protect a girl called Alex, who is at risk of kidnap/death because her dad is a vital witness in a court case.

In the movie Miley's love interest, Nicholas Dexter, was played by British actor Josh Bowman. Their kissing scenes weren't at all romantic, as Miley explained to *OK! Magazine*: 'People have a hard time thinking about it as not being romantic, but it's really not. Someone comes in and powders you or him and it's not attractive even though you're all made up but when you kiss and someone yells, "Hold it longer. Use tongue! Tongue her!"... It's weird and embarrassing. You're kind of numb to it and it doesn't bother you anymore.'

DID YOU KNOW?

Josh Bowman used to date 'Back to Black' singer Amy Winehouse.

Miley enjoyed filming the scenes in the sorority with all the female cast members but it made her realise that living with lots of women would drive her crazy. She wasn't afraid to do her own stunts but Billy Ray didn't like it one bit when she was dangling off the side of a building for one scene. He would have much preferred it if she had left it to one of the stuntwomen to do instead.

Miley decided to treat herself to a new tattoo and chose to have a pair of crossed arrows on the back of her right elbow. She visited legendary tattoo artist Kat Von D for the Native American-inspired tattoo. Afterwards Kat Von D tweeted, 'Simple symbols of friendship make beautiful tattoos. <3'

Miley and Liam decided to take a well-deserved break in Costa Rica at the end of January to celebrate Liam turning twenty-three on 13 January; they had had such a busy 2012 and needed to spend some quality time together. They wanted to escape for a while but the paparazzi managed to track them down and took photos of them cuddling on the beach and playing in the ocean. They were on holiday with Liam's brother Luke, his wife Samantha and their children, Holly, Ella and Harper Rose.

While in Costa Rica, Miley couldn't help but try some outdoors yoga and tweeted, 'Rare 2 get a moment to thank the universe for all my blessings in the form of yoga in a place like this.'

Luke and Samantha really enjoyed holidaying with Miley because she is so down-to-earth. He told *Entertainment Weekly*, 'She's great. She loves our kids, and our kids absolutely love her. She won our hearts. I find her really interesting. I find her very articulate, and years in maturity above her age. But at the same time, she's very much like Liam. I think a lot of people don't realize that they are really, really in love. They actually are a perfect match in a lot of ways.'

DID YOU KNOW?

When asked by a journalist which part of her life she felt most satisfied with, Miley chose her relationship with Liam.

When Miley and Liam got back from their holiday, they had to start working again. Miley really wanted to build the hype for her new album. It wasn't going to be released until October but she was releasing her first single from it in June and she really wanted people to be impressed with her new direction.

But she didn't want to start saying negative things about other artists just to cause controversy and actually applauded Ke$ha, Lady Gaga, Katy Perry and Rihanna in interviews for all being different. Miley strongly believes there is enough room for everyone in the charts and isn't the type to start hating her competition. She considers Katy Perry to be a good friend and isn't going to let anything get in the way of that.

DID YOU KNOW?

Miley can't stand it when artists try to copy other artists just because they are successful. She believes everyone should bring something fresh and unique.

Miley felt really angry when celebrity blogger Perez Hilton posted an article suggesting that she could have been cheating on Liam with *Gossip Girl* actor Ed Westwick. Perez wrote, 'Did the Mileybird just up and decide it was time to bounce on fiancé Liam Hemsworth??'

Miley was less than amused, tweeting, '@perezhilton what happened to your promise to spread love not lies. And to be a decent human being with values and morals??? Dude u ask.'

She decided to crash the filming of Tiffany Foxx's music video for 'Twisted' just for fun. Tiffany and Lil' Kim, who collaborated on the track, were shocked when she arrived on set. Miley and Lil' Kim had been speaking on Twitter but the two artists had no idea that Miley wanted to join in and they happily agreed that she could have a cameo in the video, which centred around a wild house party.

The whole vibe of the 'Twisted' video was about letting your hair down and enjoying being young – something that Miley loves to do. Indeed the party got so wild that the owner of the house that had been hired was not happy. By appearing in the video, Miley was giving Tiffany Foxx's music a real boost because the second it appeared on YouTube her Smilers wanted to check it out.

DID YOU KNOW?

Miley filmed a teaser clip for Kaptn's track 'Juice'. In the clip she takes part in a drinking challenge at an outrageous house party. However, when the official video was released, Miley didn't appear.

Miley also collaborated with Snoop Dogg on his track 'Ashtrays and Heartbreaks', which was released on 4 April, charting at number 1 on the US Reggae Digital Songs chart. It was included on his album *Reincarnated*. In the song Miley sings the hook.

CHAPTER SIXTEEN
CAN'T STOP

M iley was looking forward to attending the Oscars on 24 February 2013 at the Dolby Theatre in Hollywood but with a week to go she was really suffering with a bad migraine. She had had a hectic few weeks; she'd been working hard in the studio putting the finishing touches to her album and had also been to New York Fashion Week.

DID YOU KNOW?

Miley even spent Valentine's Day at the Marc Jacobs Collection show with her mum and supermodel Cara Delevingne.

With two days to go, Liam attended the Grey Goose pre-Oscars party at the Chateau Marmont. He was joined by

Taylor Lautner, Tobey Maguire, Josh Hartnett and many more top actors and actresses. The gossip site HollywoodLife claimed that Liam had got into a car with *Mad Men* actress January Jones at the end of the night. Various gossip sites suggested that Liam had cheated on Miley but no statement was released.

Miley also went out but she attended photographer Mario Testino's pre-Oscars party. She had a great night alongside reality star Kim Kardashian and supermodels Gisele Bündchen and Naomi Campbell at the event which marked the opening of Testino's new art gallery.

The next night was Oscars Night and Miley wasn't going to miss Elton John's legendary AIDS Foundation Academy Awards Viewing Party, held at the Pacific Design Center in West Hollywood. She wore a backless floor-length white gown by Azzaro, Givenchy pumps and diamond bracelets by Lorraine Schwartz. In the past she had attended the event with Liam but for the 2013 party she took her mum along as her date. As soon as they were inside Miley and Tish were joined by Kelly Osbourne and Kim and Kourtney Kardashian. Miley tweeted a fun photo of Elton getting a kiss from herself and Kelly, with the message, 'Love This!'

Meanwhile, the tabloids wouldn't stop talking about Liam and January Jones, which must have been hard for Miley to take. She had stopped wearing her engagement ring for a couple of days, which lead to more sensationalised stories being written about her. Miley let her Smilers know she was having a bad time by tweeting, 'I am so sick of La. And sick of the lies that come with it. I didn't call off my wedding. Taking a break from social media. #draining.

'Not discussing anything but my music from now on... My new music is gonna shut everyone up.'

Miley wanted to get back to having fun and shared a video of herself dancing and twerking to J Dash's track 'Wop'. She was wearing a unicorn onesie at the time, which made it hard to tell that it was her because she had the hood up until the very end. If you haven't seen it yet, go to YouTube and search for 'Miley Cyrus unicorn twerk video'.

Miley hadn't been planning on shooting the video and it was shot against a white background using her phone. She'd just finished a photo shoot and had decided to wear her onesie rather than getting dressed into her own clothes; she had an urge to dance and asked her friend to record her.

As soon as the video was posted it became a huge hit with Smilers and non-Smilers alike. It quickly went viral and became a massive hit worldwide, viewed more than 6 million times. Miley was stoked, telling Ryan Seacrest on his radio show, 'I can't believe how many people think I'm good at twerking – which is dope – like my life goal has been accomplished... I thought it was so weird, but I'm glad that everyone understands my humour.

'You can't really explain [twerking]... It's something that comes naturally... It's a lot of booty action.'

Miley then went back to see Kat Von D and had a heart tattoo added to her left arm. The tattoo was based on Leonardo da Vinci's groundbreaking anatomical hearts so is extremely lifelike. Only a highly skilled tattooist like Kat Von D would attempt such a complex and intricate design. Kat Von D tweeted, 'Just did the RADDEST tattoo on

@MileyCyrus – a miniature rendition of a daVinci anatomical heart! ❤

'This was a challenging and seriously fun tattoo for me to do.'

HollywoodLife tried to come up with a new angle on their Liam/Miley-split story and posted two articles claiming that Miley had met with Nick Jonas for lunch. Their 'source' was very vague and said, 'They seemed to be having a business meeting – they were on their phones and then they left without incident.'

Miley soon revealed that the 'source' must have been lying when she tweeted, 'I literally haven't seen Nick Jonas in years. Don't believe everything you read folks.

'Why are magazines allowed to publish straight bull sh*t. Look at my profile pic. Look at my finger. Idiots. I couldn't have "ran" into anyone because I haven't been to eat out in public in weeks because of the amount of paparazzi outside my house. #shorthairrapunzel.'

Miley and Liam seemed to have got things back on track a few weeks later. In April *Elle* magazine published an interview where Miley was asked about Liam. She replied, 'We have a house together and dogs. It just seems right to be wearing this ring and to be committed. But we keep our relationship low-key and don't talk about it anymore.

'We were too nice to the world and gave them too much insight – into my life and my puppies and my house – and I just don't feel they get that privilege anymore.

'Like on my Twitter, I'm much more… not conservative, but you don't see a picture of my dogs. You don't get that personal stuff anymore.'

They didn't reveal when Miley had given the interview so Smilers weren't sure if it took place before the Oscars or afterwards.

Her dad was asked by *Nightline* on 16 April whether he thought they would get married. Billy Ray replied, 'I don't know. I play it by ear, and I know whatever's meant to be, that's the way it's gonna happen.

'They're young. They're kids. The great news is they're great friends. They're really, really good friends. And if you end up getting married, that's your business too, you know?'

In May, Miley celebrated winning the top spot on *Maxim*'s Hot 100 list, claiming the title from 2012 winner model Bar Refaeli. She shared the news with her fans by joining Instagram and posting up a photo taken by the *Maxim* photographer. Miley had changed her mind about posting up personal photos and shared a few pictures of her dogs.

She also teased her fans by tweeting, 'Maybe y'all will find out a LIL sum at the up coming @billboard music awards! Maybe…. Like…. A…. Singgggg….lllleeeee.'

The Billboard Music Awards were held on 20 May at the MGM Grand Garden Arena in Las Vegas. Miley had been wanting to share her new music with the world for so long that she was extra-excited to perform it for the first time. She wanted people to love the song but thought that, even if they didn't, she would still love it herself. She confessed to *Billboard*, 'I didn't make this song for the critics, but for the people living it… I'm twenty years old and I want to talk to the people that are up all night with their friends. It's based on a true story of a crazy night I had: when I heard the song for the first time, it captured exactly what I was living.'

Miley was thrilled when 'We Can't Stop' was released on 3 June. She had loved every second of recording the video, which was a wild party with lots of butt shaking, huge bears, girls and crazy things happening. It was a grown-up version of 'Party in the USA', with references to twerking and drug use. She had planned for the video to be wilder but some of the scenes had to be cut; in it she gets spanked but originally she was spanking too.

Miley's main outfit for the video had been inspired by her friend and producer Pharrell Williams, who had said, 'It's not what you're wearing, it's the way you wear it.' She didn't need to wear a stereotypical sexy outfit to be sexy, she could wear anything and her attitude would make it sexy. Miley confessed to *Harper's Bazaar*, 'I feel like every girl is trying to have a beauty shot and prove that they're "fashion." But I can be in white leggings and a white sports bra and I'm on a whole other level of sh*t that those girls don't even get yet because they don't know how to do it.'

After she released the video she received a very special tweet from one of her heroes, Britney Spears. Britney wrote, 'Loving your new video for #WeCantStop! Maybe you can teach me how to twerk sometime LOL.'

Miley replied, 'We could twerk it out in exchange for u teaching me da moves 2 "slave for you" (I've been practicing for the past 10 years.)'

Miley's video for 'We Can't Stop' couldn't have been more different from her *Hannah Montana* videos. She explained to the *Daily Star Sunday*, 'I don't think I've ever had to exorcise Hannah because I think people knew I was different from her in real life... Most people on Disney act as if they are really like their characters but I never felt the need to do that. I never pretended I was as good as what Disney writes.

'They try to make someone not grow up but you can't do that to real, normal people... If I'm doing something I'm going to do it right but then once I'm away from it I'll do it my way.'

'We Can't Stop' had originally been earmarked for Rihanna but she didn't end up hearing it because she had decided on her single 'Pour It Up' before the song's producer Mike WiLL Made It got a chance to play it to her. The lyrics really meant something to Miley because she believes 'we can love who we want'.

He told MTV, 'She [Miley] liked it, so I thought we were going to knock out one record, and we ended up going in, caught a good vibe, and she's a real cool, regular person.

'We went in, she nailed the record, and she did it with her swag. So it sounds totally different than from what we originally tried to come up with.'

Miley insisted to *Rolling Stone* that the 'dancing with Molly' line from her song was not a reference to the drug Ecstasy. She told the magazine, 'I knew people were gonna wonder what I'm saying in that song... I have an accent, so when I say, "Miley", it must sound like "Molly". You're not allowed to say "Molly" on the radio, so it obviously says, "Miley".

'Have you heard [rapper Rick Ross's "Believe It" lyric] "I got a bad b**ch in my Chevy/Sellin' Miley Cyrus in my brand-new Monte Carlo"? People refer to [cocaine] as "Miley Cyrus"... so even if I'm saying "Miley" [on my song], people could find something wrong with it.'

After promoting the single as much as possible, Miley had time for a short break and decided to chill in the Bahamas. Although spotted by a few fans she didn't mind taking the odd fan photo. She had been ridiculously busy promoting 'We Can't Stop' on *Jimmy Kimmel Live in Los Angeles* one day, then flying to New York to promote it on *Good Morning America*. She'd done so many interviews that it was hard to keep track of exactly how many.

DID YOU KNOW?

Some people tried to say that Miley was imitating Nicki Minaj but she denied it. She would never try to copy another performer.

When Jay-Z mentioned Miley in his track 'Somewhere in America', it showed how iconic Miley's twerking had become. Jay-Z might have been poking fun at her, but that didn't matter.

He was asked by a fan via Twitter, 'You really think Miley Cyrus is still twerking somewhere in America?' and he replied, 'yes! she represents an old worlds worst nightmare.

'Black neighbor, and the daughter not seeing color.'

Miley decided to speak out after receiving negative tweets about her twerking. She tweeted, 'Call it what you want. But I don't see Mr. Carter shoutin any of you bitches out. #twerkmileytwerkMiley

'Exactly right. I am an old worlds worst nightmare. #outwiththeold #inwiththenewnew.'

Miley had to promote 'We Can't Stop' all around the world. When in London, she told the *Sunday People*, 'All I do is work so I eat to keep me going... I'm always on the road so I eat healthily as I have to give my body what it needs. If you don't you will crash and burn.

'The s***** part about my travels is that I don't get to work out. I do yoga and ten salutes to the sun every day then I do thirty push ups, I try to do quick things – not to stay in shape but to get my mind right.'

She wasn't happy with the way MTV UK edited her video before showing it and, when the *Sunday People* asked for her response to those who say it is too provocative, she replied, 'Then I'll give you an edit. I just think the world is so lame because you can shoot people in a movie and you can let people like [George] Zimmerman off on trial but you can't have someone going like this [she mimed an oral sex gesture], that is so dumb to me... The world is such a f***ed up place the last thing people need to worry about is my cute little video for "We Can't Stop", you know what I mean?'

Miley might have been feeling annoyed but she was soon grinning from ear to ear when she found out that she had obliterated a VEVO record. 'We Can't Stop' had been viewed 100 million times, making it the first video ever to have done so in such a short period of time. She tweeted, 'We got 100 million views?!?!?!... We did it! We broke the vevo record! 100 million views in 37 days maaaafakkkkas!!!! Directors cut coming soon!'

Miley had promised fans that, if they managed to break the record, she would share a new version of the video. She had lost out to One Direction a few days earlier when they beat her VEVO record for the most views in 24 hours. 'Best Song Ever' was viewed 10.9 million times, just slightly more than Miley's 'We Can't Stop', which had been viewed 10.7 million times.

The director's-cut version of the video was a big hit with fans. They thought that the director, Diane Martel, had really captured something special. Miley agreed, telling MTV about how they got the green light to do what they wanted. She said, 'Me and Diane had this vision that you couldn't really explain to people. They just had to trust you and I kind of said, "Trust me on this one thing and, if this is the best thing that's ever happened to me, you just know you'll have to continue to trust me. And if not, you never have to trust me again."

'Since it's done so well, and now it's at a hundred million [views] and we've got this crazy director's cut and fans have been loving it so much, and the video has done exactly what I wanted it to do, which was kind of take over the Internet and go viral and be something different and fun.'

DID YOU KNOW?
Diane Martel also directed the 'Blurred Lines' video for Robin Thicke.

'We Can't Stop' was a smash hit around the world. It was number 1 in the UK and New Zealand, number 2 in America, number 3 in Canada and Norway, number 4 in Australia and number 5 in Spain and Sweden. Miley was extremely happy that Smilers liked her new direction and she couldn't wait to release her next single.

CHAPTER SEVENTEEN
RIDING HIGH

As well as promoting her own music, Miley was still keen to help other artists. She collaborated with her producer friend Mike WiLL Made It on his first single, '23', alongside Wiz Khalifa and Juicy J.

Miley explained how she came to get involved. She said, 'He [Mike WiLL Made It] had had this track "23" with Wiz and Juicy already, and it's just on some cool, like, old-school J sh** and that's what's really cool about it... And like people wouldn't expect me to be on a song about Jordan... right now all they really see of me and Juicy is me at his concert way too twerked up, they haven't seen what we can do when we're together and when we're together it's this crazy kind of vibe because it's not what people would really expect.'

She also worked with rapper French Montana on a remix of his track 'Ain't Worried About Nothin'. However, she received lots of negative tweets when the song was released because Montana uses the 'n-word' several times. Miley didn't say it herself but this didn't stop the haters sending her abuse. She tweeted in response, 'i know what color my skin is… you can stop with the friendly reminders bitch.' She also tweeted a picture with the lyrics from 'We Can't Stop': 'It's my mouth I can say what I want to.'

DID YOU KNOW?

In July 2013 Miley posed naked for a Marc Jacobs' T-shirt campaign to raise money for the New York Skin Cancer Institute.

Miley might have missed the 2012 Teen Choice Awards to be with Liam but they both wanted to be at the 2013 event. She wore an outfit by Yves Saint Laurent – a fishnet shirt with a leather bra, a leather mini-skirt and white platforms. Miley was picking up the Candie's Fashion Trendsetter Award, the Choice TV Scene Stealer Award (for *Two and a Half Men*) and the Choice Summer Song for 'We Can't Stop'. Liam wasn't there to pick up any awards himself but he was presenting two of the acting awards, to Rebel Wilson and Skylar Astin.

When Miley collected her Teen Choice surfboard for winning the Candie's Fashion Trendsetter Award, she told the audience what it means to her to win an award for fashion. She said, 'You know, to be a trendsetter you have to have an amazing group of people that follow your trends, so I want to thank all my fans for following me and being inspired and for being so original and different... That's what fashion is really all about. I urge you guys to always be different.'

In her acceptance speech for the Choice Summer Song Award she called Liam her boo. She said, 'I have to start off, of course, thanking my amazing fans, my Smilers, for making this happen for me... Of course, Mike WiLL Made It, who put me on the map with "We Can't Stop" and my Made It Mafia family. Everyone on my label, my team... My fam, my friends, my boo – everyone that's made this happen for me. This is so amazing. So thank you, guys, so much. Can't stop, won't stop!'

Miley really wanted to promote Liam's latest movie, *Paranoia*, so, when it was released on 16 August, she tweeted, 'Go see @ParanoiaMovie the lead actor @LiamHemsworth is pretty cute.'

DID YOU KNOW?

Liam might have had a Twitter account himself but he wasn't into posting lots of personal info or photos of himself looking buff. Miley liked bragging about how gorgeous he was but Liam himself had a ban on 'shirtless selfies'.

Miley decided to add to her tattoo collection and choose to have a tooth-bone tattoo added to her right arm and 'Rolling $tone' to the bottom of her feet. She decided to get the *Rolling Stone*-inspired tattoo for fun and because she wanted to commemorate her first cover for the magazine.

'People get tattoos of the most f*****-up shit,' she told them.

'Did you know Alec Baldwin has Hannah Montana's initials tattooed on him? No, wait – Stephen Baldwin. He said he was my biggest fan, and I told him my biggest fans have tattoos. So he got hm tattooed on his shoulder... People do f*****-up shit.'

CHAPTER EIGHTEEN

SHOCKING
THE WORLD

Miley was very excited about the MTV Video Music Awards, tweeting fans a photo of herself licking one of the awards that would be given out on 25 August 2013. She told MTV as she shot a promo for the awards show, 'It's going to be super-dope when I win my VMA, my Moonman, 'cause one, I already made out with him, so now he has to go home with me... And the other thing that I think my fans are obviously so crazy... and I'm always a big believer that your word is your wand so, if I put any ifs, it's unsure if I'm gonna get it, or not. If I just say "I am", hopefully the Smilers make that happen but, if not, I already held him and I already got my picture with him, so I just gonna tell people I won even if I didn't.'

Miley was up for three awards: Best Female Video, Best

Editing and Best Song of the Summer with 'We Can't Stop'. Her whole focus, though, was on her performance, which she hoped would go down in VMA history. She didn't want it to be in the top-20 performances ever, or even the top-10… she wanted it to be number 1. After all she had put in so many hours rehearsing with her dancers to make sure everything was slick; she wanted it to be a thousand times better than her video; she wanted people to feel that they were taking part in the video itself.

Miley told fans that her date was her 'Boo' but instead of it being Liam, it was a giant teddy bear. She shared some photos of the teddy and confessed that she would be revealing her new album's cover art very soon.

Miley's outfit for the red carpet at the VMAs was a 1992 Dolce & Gabbana piece. She loved how it was from the year she was born. For her performance she wore a teddy-bear corset before taking it off to reveal a skin-coloured latex bra and pants.

DID YOU KNOW?

Miley can't fully understand why people can be so negative when she wears her stage outfits but she thinks it has a lot to do with them being scared of her self-confidence. She isn't the type of woman to conform and she doesn't care what people think. When people tell her she's sexy, she can't help but say thank you: she feels honoured that they think that.

Miley certainly gave her Smilers and the wider world something to talk about. Lady Gaga might have ended her

VMA opening performance of 'Applause' wearing a very skimpy shell bikini but it was Miley's performance of 'We Can't Stop' with Robin Thicke that will go down in history.

Miley started her high-energy performance emerging from the belly of a giant teddy bear. She danced and twerked with her dancers, who were dressed as teddy bears. She sang 'We Can't Stop' before Robin Thicke arrived on the stage and together they performed his hit 'Blurred Lines'. She bent over and gyrated with a foam finger, touching herself and Robin. As Robin stood directly behind her she made several sexual references; she even licked his neck as he sang.

While the MTV VMAs aired, Miley's performance was tweeted about more than any other – an incredible 306,000 tweets were sent per minute. There were three times as many tweets about Miley than there had been for the whole of the 2012 awards show. In total she was mentioned 4.5 million times. Miley might have performed 'We Can't Stop' but it made downloads of her new single 'Wrecking Ball' go through the roof. The second single from her *Bangerz* album had only been released that day.

Some people called Miley's performance a freak show and criticised her for having black women as her back-up dancers, midgets and 6ft 7in Amazon Ashley twerking. They wrongly thought that Miley was using them as props. Her costume designer, Lisa Katnic, told *The Cut*: 'I feel bad for people who had to watch the performance on-camera. It was a spectacle in person.

'Somebody said that it was racist for a white girl to have three black girls as props onstage to benefit herself... It's misinformed because [those dancers] L.A. Bakers are in the

["We Can't Stop"] video. At this point, Miley and the L.A.
Bakers are friends, and Amazon Ashley? They're friends in
real life. They go out to lunch.'

DID YOU KNOW?

The inventor of the foam finger was upset by the
gestures Miley made and said she had degraded an
icon.

Miley's performance was also criticised by one of the
midgets who had performed onstage with her. Hollis Jane
wrote in her blog, 'I had never been in a performance where
I was purely meant to be gawked or laughed at... I will never
forget that performance because it is what forced me to
draw my personal line in the sand... I love being the center
of attention, but that was something different. I was being
stared and laughed at for all of the wrong reasons. I was
being looked at as a prop... as something less than human.'

Hollis had been invited to go on tour with Miley but
decided not to because of how she felt. She didn't hold
anything against the 'little people' who were happy to be in
Miley's show but it wasn't for her.

Miley found it strange that she herself was criticised loads
but that Robin Thicke walked away pretty much scot-free.
People just took her performance at face value and didn't
look any deeper. Her teddy bears had been designed by artist
Todd James and there were fake Picasso paintings by the
stage but hardly anyone noticed them.

DID YOU KNOW?

Robin Thicke was asked in an interview with Oprah Winfrey whether his dance moves with Miley were sexual. He seemed to blame Miley, saying, 'Well, I was onstage, [so] I didn't see it...

'So to me, I'm walking out toward Miley, I'm not thinking sex, I'm thinking fun... I'm singing my butt off. I'm singing and I'm looking at the sky and I'm singing and I'm not really paying attention to all that. That's on her.'

Miley's friends decided to defend her in a series of tweets they sent the day after her MTV VMA performance. Former *American Idol* winner Kelly Clarkson had tweeted, 'Just saw a couple performances from the VMA's last night. 2 words.... #pitchystrippers.'

Miley's friend, celebrity blogger Dominic Riccitello, was fuming and tweeted, 'Kelly Clarkson called Miley a pitchy stripper. Do you think she's mad because her last few singles flopped and she wasn't asked to perform.'

Miley's best friend, Cheyne Thomas, seemed even angrier, tweeting, '@DominicScott and she's fat and 30... the reasons Kelly Clarkson is bitter could really go on for a day...'

Miley's new manager, Larry Rudolph, couldn't have been happier with her VMA performance and the buzz it created. She had moved to Larry in 2012 after saying goodbye to her long-term manager, Jason Morey. Larry is best known for managing Britney Spears but he had also managed Will.i.am, Nicole Scherzinger and Justin Timberlake.

Miley and her family were happy with her performance too and they decided to ignore the negative news articles written about her in the days that followed. Even if Miley had regretted it, she wouldn't have apologised because she learns from every experience. In her MTV documentary *Miley: The Movement*, which aired on 2 October, she revealed, 'I don't pay attention to the negative... I've seen this play out so many times. How many times have we seen this play out in pop music? Madonna's done it. Britney's done it. Every VMA performance, that's what you're looking for, you're wanting to make history.'

DID YOU KNOW?

In the aftermath of the VMAs Miley and Justin Bieber released a new song together called 'Twerk'. It was a club track, only two and a half minutes long. In it Miley sings, 'I came up in this party time to twerk!' It's a fun track and well worth checking out on YouTube if you haven't seen it. They had recorded it months before the VMAs with Justin's friend Lil Twist and producer Maejor Ali.

Gossip bloggers posted stories claiming Liam had been disgusted by the performance and the engagement was off but no official statement was released by Liam or Miley. Lots of people also started poking fun of Miley and her tongue after the VMAs but she took it all in good humour. Sticking out her tongue became her trademark and she would later slide down a giant tongue at the opening of her Bangerz concerts.

> **DID YOU KNOW?**
>
> Miley really wishes she could touch her nose with her tongue or do tricks but she can't. She started sticking it out when posing for photos because she finds having her photo taken embarrassing.

Smilers were left speechless when they saw Miley's video for 'Wrecking Ball', which was released on 9 September. Directed by Terry Richardson, the hauntingly beautiful video couldn't have been more different to the video for 'We Can't Stop'. In it Miley is astride a swinging wrecking ball, smashing walls and licking a sledgehammer. It was a sexual video, thanks to Miley being naked apart from a pair of boots, but also showed her vulnerable side. Her eyes are full of despair and sadness as she sings. Filming it was very emotional for Miley as she finds crying in front of people really hard.

> **DID YOU KNOW?**
>
> To make herself look so upset and distraught Miley pictured her dog Lila. She still misses her every day so it wasn't hard to cry.

Originally Miley was only supposed to look at the sledge-hammer and not kiss it but when director Terry Richardson told her to pretend she was in love with it, she couldn't help but get her tongue out. The crew were concerned because the sledgehammer was painted but Miley didn't care. She licked and kissed it because she thought it would really add something great to the final video.

Some people wrongly thought that Billy Ray would have a problem with Miley stripping off for the video but he didn't. Billy Ray will always be his daughter's number-one fan, no matter what she does. He thought 'Wrecking Ball' was an amazing song and told *Entertainment Tonight*, 'It wouldn't have mattered if Miley would have worn jeans and a flannel shirt, a tux or a nun's habit – her performance vocally on the tune reflects her roots and sheer God-given talent.'

A few weeks earlier he had been asked by *Entertainment Tonight* what he thought of her VMA performance and had answered, 'She's still my little girl and I'm still her dad, regardless how this circus we call show business plays out. I love her unconditionally and that will never change.'

Miley had been stoked when the 'We Can't Stop' video set a VEVO record for the fastest time a video has got to 100 million views but she was ecstatic when 'Wrecking Ball' obliterated this. 'We Can't Stop' had taken 37 days, whereas 'Wrecking Ball' had only taken 6 days. Miley was on cloud nine. She tweeted, 'Wrecking Ball broke the record! #100million #certified GO CELEBRATE TONIGHT #SMILERZ I love you more than anything in the world.'

She encouraged them to keep watching the video, tweeting, 'Lets get to 150 million #vevo #wreckingball #directorscut.'

'Wrecking Ball' was a huge hit around the world. It was number 1 in the USA, UK, Albania, Canada, Hungary, Israel, Lebanon, Mexico and Spain, number 2 in Australia, Austria, the Czech Republic, France, Greece, Ireland, New Zealand and Norway, and number 3 in Italy, Luxemburg and Sweden.

DID YOU KNOW?
Miley always knew 'Wrecking Ball' would be massive but one of the song's producers, Dr. Luke, wasn't so confident and didn't think it would top the charts in the USA. For a joke, Miley bet him a Numi toilet that it would, which is a pricey bet as the designer toilets cost $10,000 each.

In September representatives from both Miley and Liam confirmed to *People* magazine that they had split up. Only a day later, Liam was photographed passionately kissing Mexican actress/singer Eiza Gonzalez in Beverly Hills. They had been photographed clubbing together in Las Vegas just a few days earlier.

Smilers were shocked that Liam could move on so quickly. They flooded Miley with positive tweets and her own mum retweeted the message, '2013 = Miley's year.' Later on she tweeted, 'I love how GODS plan is ALWAYS perfect!'

Miley didn't comment on the photos of Liam and Eiza and instead promoted the MTV Europe Music Awards, which were taking place in Amsterdam on 10 November. She was nominated for three awards: Best Video for 'Wrecking Ball', Best Female and Best Pop. She was focusing on her music and tweeted, '#1 on Billboard. #1 on iTunes. #1 on Spotify. #1 on Streaming. #1 on Digital songs. #1 most added to pop radio. #1 on VEVO. #WreckingBall ❤'

Miley had stopped following Liam on Twitter, which showed that she was moving on with her life and looking to the future. She tweeted, 'Just wanted to say I love you to all my fans. Not only because of this incredible week with #WreckingBall (THANK YOU) but just because.... ❤'

In the days that followed, the press tried to suggest that Miley had moved on too and was dating her producer friend Mike WiLL Made It. All she had done was hug Mike in public after he had come to Las Vegas to support her as she performed at the iHeart Radio Music Festival.

A spokesperson for Miley told *E! News*, 'They have been spending a lot of time together because they are working so closely together on [Miley's] album. [They work] closely professionally and it is all about the music.'

Mike couldn't believe that there were dating rumours about himself and Miley. He tweeted, 'Crazy how u can make something out of nothing.' He then retweeted a link to a news article that confirmed there was nothing going on between them. But the press wouldn't leave Miley alone and a week later linked her to another of her friends, this time Juicy J. Miley thought it was hilarious and tweeted, 'waking up to the news that I'm now pregnant with @therealjuicyj baby.' She joked with Cheyne that she would obviously call the baby 'Juicy J Jr'.

DID YOU KNOW?
Whenever Miley goes through tough break-ups, she tries to look on the bright side of life and keep smiling. She has revealed in the past that when she's feeling down, she reads her Bible and this helps. After one break-up she tweeted, 'Talking to the one man who keeps his promise. One man who really understands "unconditional love" – Jesus.'

CHAPTER NINETEEN
BANGERZ

Miley was happy being single and wasn't about to rush into another relationship. She was enjoying being able to do exactly what she wanted all the time and just being on her own. Of course she wouldn't be single forever but she wasn't ready to start dating again just yet. She sent a number of updates on Twitter, telling fans how happy she was. She tweeted, 'I'm exhausted from being so f***ing happy. In bed at 9:45 & it feels so good.

'Eating mangos in bed. I repeat... happiest girl in the world.'

And she got a new tattoo – a picture of her 'Mammie' – underneath her heart tattoo on 4 November 2013. She tweeted a photo of the tattoo with the message, 'Because I am her favorite & she is mine.'

Getting people excited about her *Bangerz* album being released was top priority for Miley, but when she read an open letter that Irish singer-songwriter Sinéad O'Connor had written to her, she felt she had to respond. Miley had told various interviewers that her 'Wrecking Ball' video close-ups had been inspired by those in Sinéad's legendary 'Nothing Compares 2 U' video, which made Sinéad want to offer Miley some advice.

In her letter Sinéad writes,

I am happy to hear I am somewhat of a role model for you and I hope that because of that you will pay close attention to what I am telling you.

I am extremely concerned for you that those around you have led you to believe, or encouraged you in your own belief, that it is in any way 'cool' to be naked and licking sledgehammers in your videos.

It is in fact the case that you will obscure your talent by allowing yourself to be pimped, whether it's the music business or yourself doing the pimping.

It is absolutely NOT in ANY way an empowerment of yourself or any other young women, for you to send across the message that you are to be valued (even by you) more for your sexual appeal than your obvious talent.

Miley was greatly angered by Sinéad's comments and, in response, compared her to troubled actress Amanda Bynes. Sinéad suffers with mental illness and Miley decided to retweet some of Sinéad's posts asking for help. She tweeted,

'Before Amanda Bynes… There was…' with a screenshot of some of Sinéad's old tweets where she'd asked to see a psychiatrist. She also posted up a photo of Sinéad ripping up a photo of the Pope on *Saturday Night Live* in protest against sexual abuse in the Catholic Church.

But Sinéad didn't take kindly to Miley's response to what she thought was a heartfelt letter and decided to write three more open letters to her. They were published on her official Facebook page and were far more aggressive than her first.

Sinéad writes, 'Miley… Really? Who the f**k is advising you? Because taking me on is even more f**kin' stupid than behaving like a prostitute and calling it feminism. You have posted today tweets of mine which are two years old, which were posted by me when I was unwell and seeking help so as to make them look like they are recent. In doing so you mock myself and Amanda Bynes for having suffered with mental health issues and for having sought help.' Threatening legal action, she wrote, 'Remove your tweets immediately or you will hear from my lawyers. I am certain you will be hearing from all manner of mental health advocacy groups also. It is not acceptable to mock any person for having suffered.

'Furthermore you posted a photo of me tearing the pope's photo… as if to imply insanity… by doing so all you have achieved is to expose your staggering ignorance.

'I suggest you read The Philadelphia Report, The Boston Report, all the reports which will illuminate for you why that action of mine remains sane and valid. By mocking it you mock every child who suffered sexual abuse at the hands of priests and had it covered by the Vatican.

'You could really do with educating yourself, that is if you're not too busy getting your tits out to read.'

The final letter read,

Miley, I have no interest in meeting you. You can take five minutes today between g-string f**kin' changes to publicly apologise and remove your abusive tweets. If you do not then you don't give a sh*t who you mock and what damage you do by being so ignorant. I have no interest in or desire to cause you trouble but if you do not apologise for having deliberately tried to cause me hurt and trouble personally and professionally I will have to bring pressure upon you. When you end up in the psych ward or rehab I'll be happy to visit you... and would not lower myself to mock you.

Bangerz was released on 4 October. The day before it came out Miley revealed on the *Today Show* that they had both put a line under the matter and moved on. She simply said,

If you want to know my thoughts, I think she's an incredible artist. I think she's an awesome songwriter and I was really inspired by her for my 'Wrecking Ball' video, which was what started the whole thing. I don't know how someone can start a fight with somebody that's saying, 'Hey, I really respect you and I really love what you did.' 'You know what? You suck!' And that was kind of crazy... But, like I said, I'm a big fan of hers and so it doesn't really matter... It's all good. You can write as many open letters as you want. That's really what blogging is. I get open letters every day; it's nothing too new for me.

During her interview Miley was asked whether she has a five-year plan. She replied, 'Not really. I'm just focused on when I get to go on tour, which is going to be next year, which I'm really excited about... My plan is focusing on right now and continuing what I'm doing because I'm the happiest I've ever been in my whole life. So I'm really happy to be here.'

After hearing Miley's reply Billy Ray tweeted, 'Wanna know how I feel as a Father? Just heard my daughter say @MileyCyrus "I'm the happiest I've ever been in my whole life". All I ever wanted.'

Bangerz stormed to the top of the album charts worldwide. It was number 1 in the USA, UK, Australia, Brazil, Canada, Ireland and Norway, number 2 in New Zealand and Spain, number 3 in Denmark, Italy and Mexico, and did well in so many other countries too.

Heather Phares wrote in her review for AllMusic, 'Brassy empowerment jams like "Maybe You're Right", "Do My Thang" and "FU" sell Cyrus as an independent woman, and the album accomplishes that mission: *Bangerz* transforms Miley into a pop star who won't – and can't – be ignored as she rings in her twenties.'

Entertainment Weekly's reviewer Nick Catucci gave the album an A-, writing,

Yes, Miley raps. And if you can't stand Ke$ha, you probably won't take to Cyrus' skills, either. Her confidante Britney Spears rhymes too, on 'SMS

(Bangerz)': 'They ask me how I keep a man/I keep a battery pack!' But it's all in Cyrus' toolbox, along with everything from mutated honky-tonk (the winningly nutty Pharrell production '4x4,' with Nelly) to shameless frat-party-starting ('Love Money Party,' featuring Big Sean paying tribute to red Solo cups). She's not only game for 'My Darlin',' a trippy duet with Auto-Tune artiste Future, she makes it a genuine weeper. And when she's handed conventional EDM club bait such as 'Someone Else,' she calls up her chops and throws into relief just how meek typical DJ bros like their hook girls.

Track Listing:
1. Adore You
2. We Can't Stop
3. SMS (Bangerz) featuring Britney Spears
4. 4x4 featuring Nelly
5. My Darlin' featuring Future
6. Wrecking Ball
7. Love Money Party featuring Big Sean
8. #GETITRIGHT
9. Drive
10. FU featuring French Montana
11. Do My Thang
12. Maybe You're Right
13. Someone Else
14. Deluxe Version (bonus tracks)
15. Rooting for My Baby
16. On My Own
17. Hands in the Air featuring Ludacris

During her VMA promo shoot for MTV Miley confided, 'I have a lot of features on my record. Big Sean and Ludacris and, of course, [Pharrell Williams] has done a bunch of my records, so I'm really excited about that… I get to work with Future, who's like my favorite kind of new artist right now, even though he's not that new now… [He] and I wrote a bunch of songs on this record together and he's featured on one of them.'

DID YOU KNOW?

Because Miley was still engaged to Liam when the album artwork went to print, her dedication includes, 'I could not have made this album without one person… FE. Thank you for inspiring me (PS. I Love You).' FE was one of Miley's nicknames for Liam.

One of the artists that Miley collaborated with on *Bangerz* was Nelly. Their track '4X4' was produced by Pharrell Williams. Before the album was released Nelly told MTV, 'It's kind of a country, hip-hop, pop feel, if you can believe that… it's about having fun, kind of how a four-by-four truck symbolises rebelliousness.

'You know, mashing out, wanting to ride with the bad boys… it's a dope track.'

Nelly is a huge fan of Miley and loves the fact that she just wants to have fun. He thinks her critics should give her a break because she's only in her early twenties; she's got plenty of time to be sensible when she's older. Miley believes now is the time for her to act like a child because when she was a child, she had to act like an adult all the time. This put her under a lot of pressure.

Miley also collaborated with none other than Britney Spears. Their track 'SMS (Bangerz)' was instantly a fan favourite. Originally, her team had suggested Gwen Stefani or Nicki Minaj as her collaborator but Miley thought Britney was perfect.

DID YOU KNOW?

When Miley was promoting *Bangerz*, she carried around a bag filled with her favourite accessories (things like gold chains, stilettos and fancy belts) so that she could use them at any photo shoots if the accessories the shoots' stylists provided weren't up to scratch. Image is very important to Miley.

Pharrell Williams is Miley's mentor as well as her producer. When they met for the first time, he was blown away by how focused she was and how determined she was to make the kind of music she wanted to make. She didn't want hit records if they weren't the right songs; she needed to be able to express herself through her music.

Miley wanted her fans to listen to the album several times to fully grasp everything she wanted it to convey. The order of the tracks is important as it shows her changing and growing. The album was about her relationship with Liam but she intentionally put 'Someone Else' at the end because it represents where she was when the record was released; Miley had evolved into a new person.

When Miley was in the studio recording, she often saw

Britney Spears because the singer was working on her new music in the same studio. Sharing the same manager, Larry Rudolph, also meant that they saw each other frequently.

DID YOU KNOW?
Miley's mum and Britney's mum are friends.

Miley loves writing her own songs but she also wants to try to write songs for other artists. In October 2013 she tweeted The Way singer Ariana Grande to tell her that she had written a song especially for her. She wrote, 'Why did I wake up and immediately write a song for @ArianaGrande... In the shower.'

Ariana was thrilled and replied, 'Omg @MileyCyrus I'm dying I want to hear... And you're coming over when I get back from London. We're neighbors after all... there's no option.'

And Miley was truly thankful to her British Smilers when she was told that 'Wrecking Ball' was at the top of the UK singles chart and *Bangerz* was at the top of the album chart at the same time. It was such a fantastic achievement because there were so many great singles and albums out at the same time.

When she had released 'Can't Be Tamed' in June 2010, it had only reached number 8 in the charts and her *Hannah Montana* albums and singles had never done particularly well in the UK. Her only other number 1 single had been 'We Can't Stop'.

DID YOU KNOW?

When Miley presented comedy show *Saturday Night Live* on 5 October, she announced that she wouldn't be playing Hannah Montana and jokingly said, 'but I can give you an update on what she's been up to – she's been murdered.'

For Halloween, Miley decided to dress up as one of her musical heroes – Lil' Kim. She chose to wear Lil' Kim's very daring purple jumpsuit from the 1999 MTV VMAs. The outfit required her to wear a purple wig and expose her left breast, with only the nipple covered. She tweeted a photo to her followers so they would be the first to know.

Lil' Kim was flattered that Miley had chosen to dress as her and told MTV, 'She did me very well. I think she looked gorgeous. I love her; she's one of my besties... She's like my bestie-slash-wifey. You know what's so funny? As soon as she tweeted the picture, she texted me and was like, she was like, "Happy Halloween, babe!"... I think she did me well.'

DID YOU KNOW?

For Halloween 2012, Miley had dressed as Nicki Minaj, wearing a leopard-print catsuit and a yellow wig. She always puts a lot of effort into her Halloween costumes.

Miley had collaborated on Future's track 'Real and True' alongside Mr Hudson and it was released on 5 November. Future had recorded 'My Darlin'' for *Bangerz* and, when

Miley heard the hook that Mr Hudson had written for Future's new track, she wanted to be involved. Future explained to *Rolling Stone*, 'She did her vocals and they sent it back to me and I wrote my verses to that and tried to come up with something unique. Her vocals are very strong and emotional on the song. She brings that passion to this record. Miley is really cool and down-to-earth; she's always fun to be around and I'm always cracking up when I'm on set with her.'

The video for 'Real and True' was released on 10 November and showed Miley dressed as an astronaut and wearing lots of silver-glitter body paint. For a section of the video she sings naked (apart from the body paint) in an observation room while Future looks on. There might be a glass window separating them but she serenades him as she sings.

DID YOU KNOW?

'Real and True' only managed to reach number 32 in the US Hot R&B chart and number 92 in the UK, which was disappointing.

Miley flew over to Amsterdam for the MTV Europe Music Awards on Sunday, 10 November (the same day the 'Real and True' video was released). She was opening the show with a performance of 'We Can't Stop' and was up for four awards.

Miley arrived early on the Thursday so she could have a nice break in the city and was spotted at The Pancake House and Greenhouse coffee shop with friends, including

Afrojack. She shared some photos on Twitter – in one of them it looked like she might have been smoking cannabis and in the other she was promoting her performance.

Miley wanted her performance at the EMAs to be just as memorable as at the VMAs. This time around she decided to incorporate aliens as well as teddy bears and didn't use any foam fingers. She enjoyed showing off her twerking skills with her midget dancers.

DID YOU KNOW?

As well as performing 'We Can't Stop', Miley performed 'Wrecking Ball' later on in the show. She wore earphones decorated with cannabis leaves.

It turned out that it wasn't Miley's performance that everyone was talking about the next day but what she did when she accepted the Best Music Video Award. Miley hadn't been planning on doing anything controversial but as she walked out of her dressing room the idea to smoke a joint as she collected her award popped into her head. She thought it would be really funny but knew that other people would have a problem with it so didn't mention it to anyone.

MTV decided to censor it when it was broadcast by panning to the audience instead of showing Miley because they knew it would create a lot of bad press, even though smoking cannabis is legal in Holland.

DID YOU KNOW?

Miley also won the Best Video Award for 'Wrecking Ball'.

She performed at the Bambi Awards on Thursday, 1 November in Berlin and then headed to the UK to sing 'Wrecking Ball' on *The X Factor*. But her performance on the British talent show wasn't up to her usual high standard and, after arriving back in Los Angeles, was told she must rest her voice. Miley had been performing so much that she needed to take a break or she could do serious damage to her throat and voice. She accepted what the doctors told her and tweeted fans to say, 'Happy to get some rest. Time to go be sicky.'

After resting for a few days Miley was ready for her performance at the American Music Awards on Sunday, 24 November. She might have turned twenty-one the day before but she couldn't celebrate until the awards ceremony was over.

Miley wanted to share her birthday weekend with her Smilers and, as a special treat, tweeted an old photo of her family. In it she is dressed as a princess and Braison is dressed likes an Indian. She tweeted on the Friday, 'I want everyone to party like its their birffffday tomorrow.' And the next day she shared a photo of her pack asleep on her bed, with the message, 'All I could want on my birthday.'

Three days after Miley's birthday a new track she had collaborated on was released. Will.i.am's 'Feelin' Myself' featured Miley and rappers Wiz Khalifa and French Montana. It was to be the lead single from Will.i.am's re-released album *#willpower*. 'Feelin' Myself' reached number 2 in the UK charts and had moderate success in other countries. It was Miley's third song with Will.i.am: they had collaborated on his song 'Fall Down', which was released on

16 April 2013, and on Miley's song 'Do Ma Thang' for her *Bangerz* album.

December was a great month for Miley. *Rolling Stone* named her album as one of the best of 2013 and *Entertainment Weekly* picked her out as one of their 'Entertainers of the Year', which was a great honour. They also picked out her mentor and producer Pharrell Williams, something Miley was more than happy about: she thinks what he did for her, Daft Punk and Robin Thicke in 2013 was incredible. She admitted to *Entertainment Weekly*,

He really feels like a brother – it's more than just us working together. No one had heard from me or him in a minute, and we were just kind of brewing up what we wanted to do next and what we wanted to drop on people. He and I were on kind of a journey together, and I couldn't be more happy for him and what he accomplished this year in everything – in fashion, in art, everything he does. There's not a better person I would wish that on. He's the best person I've ever gotten to watch and learn from. I've grown up in this industry, and I've watched a lot of people, and I think that's where I learned most of what I know. He's one of the greatest mentors I've ever had, and who he is as a person is equally as amazing as who he is as an entertainer.

Miley released her third single from her *Bangerz* album, 'Adore You', on 17 December. The video was leaked on Christmas Day and showed Miley writhing around under a bedsheet with a video camera, touching herself intimately and doing the same in a bath.

Digital Spy's Robert Copsey wrote in his review, 'The song's surprisingly stripped back – almost demo-like – production is a welcome change of pace from a singer whose tactics to take over the world previously seemed to solely rely on shock and bewilderment. "When you say you love me, know I love you more," she confesses in a gravely tone that unearths a rarely seen vulnerable side to the star. It's unlikely to convince the masses, but it's reassuring to know that even Miley Cyrus has her sombre moments.'

DID YOU KNOW?

The song only managed to reach number 21 in the US and UK charts but a remixed version by Cedric Gervais was later released.

Miley had great fun performing at the Jingle Bell Ball shows, with her dancers dressed as reindeers, Amazon Ashley as a giant Christmas tree and Cheyne as a bad Santa. She could be seen twerking on Cheyne's lap while wearing a white leotard with white furry cuffs and furry snowball earrings.

Cheyne got really angry when he thought Demi Lovato was dissing Miley in a tweet after she bumped into them both backstage at the Miami show. Demi had simply tweeted, 'You know who your friends are.'

Cheyne replied, 'So nice running into you!' to which Demi responded, 'You should come by my dressing room. Sounds super fun right?'

Cheyne continued, 'stop trying to get famous off me.'

DID YOU KNOW?

Cheyne already had some history with Demi, as he allegedly mocked her in a video on YouTube. In it he looks like he's taking a swipe at Demi for her struggle with cocaine, telling the camera, 'I can only go thirty to sixty minutes without coke,' and then swigging from a bottle of Coke.

It is such a shame that Miley and Demi are no longer good friends as they used to talk or text each other every day after Demi was in the Disney movie *Camp Rock*. There are only three months between Demi and Miley's birthdays and Demi dated Trace Cyrus for a while. Demi even gave Miley the nickname 'Dragon' because they both loved watching the movie *Step Brothers* and liked the bit when John C. Reilly's character says, 'My name is Dale but you can call me Dragon.'

On 27 December Miley and Cheyne were snapped dancing very close to one another at the Beacher's Madhouse in Las Vegas after watching a Britney Spears' show at the Planet Hollywood hotel. He was photographed touching Miley's breasts and her legs. Fans agreed that the photos looked like they were more than friends but they couldn't say for sure because both Miley and Cheyne had been drinking and it was clearly the early hours of the morning.

Miley and Cheyne didn't comment on their time in the craziest nightclub in Los Angeles but they revealed that they had loved every second of Britney's opening show earlier in the night. Miley tweeted, 'if u told me I'd be front row & center on @britneyspears opening night 10 years ago I would've never believed you.' She posted a photo of herself standing up during the show and giving a dancing Britney the thumbs up.

DID YOU KNOW?

Miley loves teasing her fans and posted a screenshot on Twitter of herself chatting to Cheyne, wearing a sexy red bra and sticking out her tongue.

On a typical night it is Miley's non-famous friends that she hangs out with, rather than her famous ones. She explained to *We Love Pop* magazine, 'I have a really weird group of friends, no one you would know. I don't hang out with super-famous people; that's not my thing.

'I hang out with the randoms. All the random LA people, they're all in the ["We Can't Stop"] video.'

CHAPTER TWENTY
FEELING THE PRESSURE

The paparazzi were out in force in January 2014, stalking Miley so badly that she felt she couldn't leave the house without getting hassled. She tweeted, 'I can't even take my dog for a walk on a Sunday.'

Later on she tweeted, 'Paps suck a fat...' and posted up a photo of an eggplant. She then added, 'Yes. Suck a fat Eggplant.'

Miley enjoys photo shoots but when she's not working, she wants to be left alone. She invited journalist Ronan Farrow into her home to interview her and posed naked in a bed for photos for the cover and to run alongside his article. The images that photographers Mert Alas and Marcus Piggott took were very risqué and several involved Miley lying in bed with two male models, exposing one of her breasts. Before the piece was published she shared one of the photos with fans, tweeting, 'Coming soon in @wmag "bed time portraits By @mertalass & @macpiggott" so xxxited check it out 2 see the real deal.'

During their interview Miley told Ronan that she's not a big fan of children, especially kids who give their parents cheek, and that she's not going to listen to critics. She chatted to him about the criticism she received for having black back-up dancers for her VMA performance and confessed, 'I don't give a s***. I'm not Disney, where they have, like, an Asian girl, a black girl, and a white girl, to be politically correct, and, like, everyone has bright-colored T-shirts. You know, it's like, I'm not making any kind of statement. Anyone that hates on you is always below you, because they're just jealous of what you have.'

But Miley had one bad habit that she wanted to stop in 2014 and that was smoking cigarettes. She tweeted in February, '2 months no cigs #proudofmyself.'

In an earlier interview with *Rolling Stone* she had put across her view that she thinks alcohol is more dangerous than weed. She confessed, 'Hollywood is a coke town, but weed is so much better. And molly, too. Those are happy drugs – social drugs. They make you want to be with friends. You're out in the open. You're not in a bathroom. I really don't like coke. It's so gross and so dark. It's like what are you, from the '90s? Ew.' Miley didn't think that smoking weed should be a problem because cannabis isn't illegal in the state of California.

People can be very quick to judge Miley but when she appeared on NBC's *The Tonight Show With Jay Leno*, she made the point that she hasn't been doing anything illegal so there are no Miley Cyrus mug shots floating around. She doesn't criticise other stars who have been in trouble with the law and offered Justin Bieber some advice while on the show: she advised him to buy a new house and get his own club built so he can party in private.

When asked to do an *MTV Unplugged* special, Miley jumped at the chance. She had to choose a special guest to sing with her and she wanted somebody that her fans wouldn't expect. Initially, she chose godmother Dolly Parton to be her special guest but she was unavailable on the day they needed to film so instead Miley decided to perform Dolly's hit 'Jolene' as a tribute to her.

Her second choice was Madonna and, thankfully, the star was available but Miley didn't get confirmation until right at the last minute. Together they sang a mash-up of Miley's 'We Can't Stop' and Madonna's 'Don't Tell Me'. The two women were very friendly during their performance, which Miley found exhilarating. She told *E! News*, 'She's the kind of person that you can do whatever you want once you're on stage… It's fun to be on stage with someone who is fearless. You don't have to think, "Oh, should I do this?" or, "Are they not going to like that?" or, "Are their people going to be mad if I do that?"'

Miley's *Unplugged* Set List:
1. 4X4
2. Do My Thang
3. #GETITRIGHT
4. SMS (Bangerz)

5. Adore You
6. Rooting For My Baby
7. Drive
8. Jolene (Dolly Parton cover)
9. Wrecking Ball
10. Don't Tell Me/We Can't Stop
11. Why'd You Only Call Me When You're High (Arctic Monkeys' cover)

DID YOU KNOW?

Miley's *MTV Unplugged* performance had the biggest ratings of any *Unplugged* episode in the last 10 years. It was viewed online 1.7 million times in the first day alone!

Miley might have been happy being single but her super-fan Matt Peterson from Arizona wanted to change that. He recorded a video asking Miley to be his prom date. It wasn't the first time she'd been asked to a prom but it was the first time she'd been asked by someone naked with only a foam finger covering his modesty. Matt had actually met Miley in person a few times, as his video montage explained. To check it out, go to YouTube and type in 'Matt Peterson Prom'. It is a really sweet video and shows Matt crying when he met Miley for the first time in 2009.

DID YOU KNOW?

Even though Miley had a tutor instead of attending school, she still attended a prom. She told *OK! Magazine*, 'High school is something I wish I would

---

have had... I still got to go to prom but it wasn't the same. Like, people bugged me for photos when I was at the prom. I went with a gay guy, and it was like the best, most fabulous night of my whole life. So I actually had a really good time when I got to go, but it was different, because it wasn't like I got asked by my high school boyfriend or anything.'

Miley couldn't attend Matt's prom because she was touring Europe but she wanted to meet him, tweeting, 'Dear Matt Peterson, I don't think I'll be able to make it to prom BUT why don't you come to my AZ show & hang w me? Don't forget a corsage.'

During the show Miley called Matt onstage and, after making him take off his customised tongue blazer, she slipped it on, leaving him in just his boxer shorts and a tie. He presented her with a beautiful corsage before they slow-danced to Miley singing 'Adore You'. It was certainly the best night of Matt's life!

DID YOU KNOW?

Whatever her critics say, Miley is a fashion icon and Marc Jacobs was happy to announce that she would be the face of his 2014 spring and summer collection. He chose her because of her great energy and natural beauty. His photographer of choice, Juergen Teller, did not wish to photograph her so he opted for photographer David Sims, who was more than happy to shoot Miley for the campaign. Their beach shoot went fantastically well, with Miley looking every inch the model. The clothes looked beautiful on her and even those who had thought Marc Jacobs was crazy to hire her couldn't deny that she did a great job.

Miley is usually the one listening to her dad's advice but she couldn't help but tell Billy Ray that he needed to take a leaf out of her book in 2014 and reinvent himself. She wanted to see him try something no one would expect of him and for Billy Ray that meant recording a new hip-hop version of 'Achy Breaky Heart' with Buck 22 (real name Damon Elliott). If people were shocked by Miley's 'Wrecking Ball' video, they would be horrified by Buck 22 and Billy Ray's new version of 'Achy Breaky Heart'. Their music video was set on a spaceship, manned by aliens (naked glamourmodels with painted faces and only tape covering their modesty). The aliens/models twerked vigorously, showing their 99-per cent naked buttocks. Miley and her track 'Wrecking Ball' did get a shout out in the 'Achy Breaky 2' video and one of the aliens bore a passing resemblance to her.

Meanwhile the press continued to link Miley with various men but she was still very much single. One of the most hurtful stories appeared in *Life & Style* magazine. Their cover story suggested that Miley had tried to seduce a boyfriend of Brandi's when she was fifteen. There was no truth in the story and the man in question, Sam Hancock, spoke out to set the record straight. He told Celebuzz, 'Not true! That's ridiculous.

'I don't want to invade Brandi's life because she's doing great things. But that never happened!'

Sam was five years older than Miley and she had never

even fancied him during the two years he was dating her sister. The magazine's source had obviously made it up.

DID YOU KNOW?

When presenter Mario Lopez asked Miley who her ideal man would be, she teased, 'Someone that doesn't really want to see me in person and someone that just likes to FaceTime... Texting relationships are the best; I love long-distance.'

Miley's outlook on men was discussed in an interview she had with W magazine. She spoke frankly about both sexes searching for the impossible, saying, 'Guys watch too much porn. Those girls don't exist. They're not real girls. And that's like us watching romance movies. That's girl porn, because, like, those guys do not exist.'

All Miley wants is a guy who loves her for who she is and is happy just to chill at home. She doesn't need big gestures or expensive dates, she just wants to find her soul mate. And she is tired of being asked in interviews about her love life and wants to concentrate on her music. Sometimes she replies bluntly when asked insensitive questions. For instance, when Love magazine asked where her engagement ring was, she simply replied, 'Don't know. Think it's in the shower.'

She did admit that she still has contact with Liam Hemsworth and hasn't cut him out of her life completely, explaining, 'We still talk and communicate. I was with him since I was sixteen and nothing's ever going to make that go away. I've known this guy all that time and if it doesn't work out I can still smile and love him and he can love me and that's great, that's the way to be. Life is too short. If you get called one day and, God forbid, that person isn't here, then the last thing you want to know [is] that you had your ego in front of you. If you love someone, tell them you do, if you want to be friends with someone, be friends with them.'

Miley is happy to choose the showbiz events she wants to attend and her label don't try and force her to go to events when she doesn't want to go. When it was the Grammys on Sunday, 26 January, she decided not to go; she was having a well-deserved break. In the morning she tweeted, 'Gonna do some serious cleaning/organizing today. My favorite way to spend a day off! #obsessivecompulsivedisorder

'Probably gonna listen to @skyferreira all day while I clean #emo.'

Miley had been busy performing '#GETITRIGHT' and Dolly Parton's 'Jolene' at Clive Davis's annual pre-Grammy gala the night before so didn't need two late nights in a row. She tweeted photos during the Grammys, showing Smilers that she was having a night in playing Guitar Hero.

CHAPTER TWENTY-ONE
SHOWTIME!

Miley was so excited about her Bangerz Tour that she was counting down the days until Valentine's Day, when she would be putting on her first show. She has never been a fan of rehearsals as they just make her more nervous, she just wanted to be out on stage, performing for her fans.

Miley deliberately chose for her tour to start on Valentine's Day because it's a depressing day for lots of people and she wanted to have the best Valentine's Day ever. She hoped that fans would enjoy the show as much as she did – she had planned everything to create the best experience she could for Smilers.

She'd hired the man behind the cartoon 'Ren & Stimpy', John Kricfalusi, and the artist Ben Jones to create amazing videos that would be shown on the giant screens as she performed. She wanted to blow people away with her strong vocals and didn't want to jeopardise that by doing lots of dancing.

Her costumes were designed by Roberto Cavalli, Jeremy Scott, the Blonds (Phillipe Blonde and his partner David Blond) and Marc Jacobs. She also wore vintage outfits by legendary designer Bob Mackie, who styled the late Judy Garland, Diana Ross and Tina Turner.

Her marijuana leotard was designed by the Blonds, who had several meetings with Miley to find out exactly what she wanted (she loves leotards that are very high-cut because they show off her long legs). She thought the leaf design was perfect for when she performed her track 'Love Money Party'. They also designed her Jessica Rabbit-style dress and the T-shirt dress she wears for the acoustic numbers.

Bangerz Tour Set List:
1. SMS (Bangerz)
2. 4x4
3. Love Money Party
4. My Darlin'
5. Maybe You're Right
6. FU
7. Do My Thang
8. #GETITRIGHT
9. Can't Be Tamed
10. Adore You
11. Drive
12. Rooting for My Baby
13. Jolene

14. Hey Ya!
15. 23
16. On My Own
17. Someone Else
18. We Can't Stop
19. Wrecking Ball
20. Party in the USA

Just days before the tour kicked off in Vancouver, Miley admitted to her sister Brandi (on *Fuse News*), 'I think my show is educational for kids... They're going to be exposed to art most people don't know about. People are taught to look at things so black and white, especially in small towns. I'm excited to take this tour to places where [art] like this wouldn't be accepted, where kids wouldn't learn about this different kind of art.'

DID YOU KNOW?

There was lots of merchandise for sale at the shows, including gold Bangerz rolling papers for $40.

Smilers and critics alike were in awe of Miley after her watching her first show. *Rolling Stone* wrote in its review, 'Miley Cyrus kicked off her much-hyped Bangerz world tour with both her immense talent and self-deprecation intact. In fact, if you approached the night as a drinking game centered around "famous Miley-isms" – extended tongues, strange singing cat animations, frottage and the like – well, you probably passed out long ago, never to remember the show. Cyrus delivered on the campy, the vampy and an assortment of other cheeky behaviors with a clear aim to distance herself ever further from the land of Hannah Montana. That said, looking past the "shock and awe," Cyrus delivered fantastic vocals all evening long.'

So many bizarre and wonderful things happened during the show. There was plenty of twerking and grinding, Miley straddled a 20-foot hot dog during her performance of 'Someone Else', which was then flown over the audience before returning to the stage. One of her dancers was dressed as a joint for 'We Can't Stop' and other dancers were lighters. In one of the videos on the big screens, Miley was shown in various stages of undress while the Alt-J track 'Fitzpleasure' was played. Some parents in the audience might have objected to the photos of Miley in bondage wear but what did they expect? She also did an acoustic set to showcase her musical range, singing 'Jolene' and Outkast's 'Hey Ya!'

Robin Syrenne from *Liberty Voice* wrote in his review, 'Miley Cyrus and her team have formulated this show to reflect exactly what they have found gets people talking without sacrificing her integrity as a vocalist, proving with the BANGERZ Tour that she really knows what she's doing.'

DID YOU KNOW?

When Miley performed 'Adore You', she asked the audience to make out and then a roving camera zoomed in on a number of couples so that their kisses could be seen by everyone on the big screens.

Just days after Miley's tour started, her concert promoter

Live Nation was forced to put out a statement after an Australian news site suggested that some dates might be pulled because Miley's show was too shocking. They told *E! News* in a statement, 'There is no truth whatsoever to any stories or rumors of venues pulling out of the Bangerz Tour. Miley has created a tour that's big, spectacular, entertaining and everything you would expect from Miley Cyrus. Reviews have been amazing and most important, fans are loving the show and having a great time.'

Miley was amused by the people who complained about her wild antics, sharing a photo of her in her marijuana leotard onstage with the 'Parent Advisory' logo clearly on display behind her on the big screen. She tweeted, 'You can't say I didn't warn you. Now sit back relax & enjoy the show. #bangerztour.

'Save your complaints for the McDonalds drive thru when they forget the "fries with that."'

Miley wanted a permanent reminder of the tour and decided it was time to visit a tattoo parlour again. She revealed a yellow crying-cat tattoo on her inner lip to her fans via Instagram, with the message, '#sadkitty #f***yeahtulsa #lovemoneyparty #freakz.'

She will never forget the crazy moments she had on tour. Miley loved entertaining her Smilers every night but she will always regret not being with her dog Floyd when he died. The pain she experienced when she heard the news was excruciating. She still managed to perform but she broke down time and time again. For Miley, her dogs and her family mean the world to her – she wouldn't be the person she is today if it wasn't for them.

Miley is so excited about what the future holds for her. She knows there will be many more ups and downs but she is determined to keep smiling no matter what!